Lessons from Iraq

Lessons from Iraq

Avoiding the Next War

Edited by
Miriam Pemberton
William D. Hartung

Paradigm Publishers

Boulder • London

Copyright © 2008 Paradigm Publishers

Published in the United States by Paradigm Publishers, 3360 Mitchell Lane, Suite E, Boulder, Colorado 80301 USA.

Paradigm Publishers is the trade name of Birkenkamp & Company, LLC, Dean Birkenkamp, President and Publisher.

Library of Congress Cataloging-in-Publication Data
Lessons from Iraq : avoiding the next war / edited by Miriam Pemberton and William D. Hartung.
    p. cm.
  Includes bibliographical references and index.
  ISBN-13: 978-1-59451-498-2 (hardcover)
  1. Iraq War, 2003—Causes.   2. United States—Politics and government—2001–
3. Political corruption—United States.   4. Iraq—Colonization.   5. Mercenary troops—
Iraq.   6. Torture—Iraq.   I. Pemberton, Miriam, 1952–   II. Hartung, William D.
  DS79.76.L47 2008
  959.7044'3—dc22

                                                                              2007046098

Printed and bound in the United States of America on acid-free paper that meets the standards of the American National Standard for Permanence of Paper for Printed Library Materials.

Designed and Typeset by Straight Creek Bookmakers.

12   11   10   09   08   1   2   3   4   5

Contents

Ways and Means

Collateral Damage .

Introduction

Miriam Pemberton

In January 2007, former senator George McGovern was in Washington to give a lunchtime speech at the National Press Club, laying out his plan for ending the U.S. war in Iraq. He spent the previous morning sitting a few blocks away in a conference room at the Institute for Policy Studies, trying out the speech on a few sympathetic friends.

The four walls of this conference room are covered by a collage of photos, book jackets, news articles, quotes, and drawings depicting IPS' involvement in the issues of four decades. On McGovern's right the cover of *The Vietnam Reader,* from 1965, looked across the room at a photo from February 15, 2003: women in Baghdad joining the millions who assembled that day in streets on every continent of the globe to oppose the Iraq war.

McGovern was in the mood to reminisce about his previous effort to end a war, the one history will remember him for. Back then his daughters worried about the toll this effort to bring U.S. troops home from Vietnam was taking on him. "You're not ending it," he recalled them saying. "Why don't you quit?" His answer was: "At least we'll never have to go down this road again." In the 2007 retelling this was a punch line, of course, and it got the laugh.

1

Such assurances, like the title of this book, have time and again been revealed to be false advertising. "Never Again" has been disproved repeatedly since it was first turned into a rallying cry: by Cambodia, Rwanda, and Darfur. Likewise, the lessons in this book will not be a guarantee against the next war, even supposing they all took hold.

There will be a next war. It needs to be undertaken only as a last resort, and the danger is great that it won't be. A necessary if insufficient way to avoid repeating the last war is to learn its lessons.

There have been many. New revelations about this war's ways and means—some officially announced, others forcibly exposed—have come at us at a relentless pace. The process of absorbing the shock of one has often been short-circuited by the onslaught of the next.

During November and December 2005, for example, we learned, first, that the Bush administration was flying terrorism suspects to secret prisons in countries that permit torture; then that, even as Secretary of State Colin Powell was making his prewar case to the United Nations about ongoing Iraqi weapons programs, U.S. intelligence agencies were raising serious doubts behind the scenes; and finally that the National Security Agency was secretly tapping Americans' phone calls without warrants.[1]

The danger is that we will absorb these shocks by getting used to them. We'll lift our burden of resistance by incorporating the unacceptable into the domain of the normal, and move on. But we can't move on. The damage done by this war has to be examined if it is to be repaired.

This book is an effort to fix some points. Nail a few things down. Declare some policies and practices off-limits to U.S. policymakers.

If what is shaping up to be the worst foreign policy disaster in U.S. history has an upside, it is: that this war should definitively, permanently settle a handful of critical questions about U.S. conduct in the world. This book tries to name them.

Settling these questions is certainly a work in progress. The Iraq war is bleeding conceptually into the limitless Global War on Terror, primarily through the Bush administration's determination to conflate the two. In the summer of 2007, as Congress failed once again to end the war, it also expanded the government's power to eavesdrop on the phone calls of Americans, without their knowledge and without a court's consent. A majority of our legislators apparently calculated, at least temporarily, that because a future terrorist attack in the United States is possible (as it will ever be, President George W. Bush's declared intentions to "defeat terrorism" notwithstanding), resistance to this violation of our civil liberties was politically impossible.

On the other hand, the American public has felt the war's damage deeply enough that this may be the most seizable moment since the end of the cold war to hash out, fight for, and solidify some principles of prevention. It's the moment to agree on some causes of the damage and remove them from the table.

All societies need a ready reference handbook that draws some lines around its conduct of war, establishing: if we're going to war, we can't do it this way, and not for these reasons. The UN Charter laid down broad outlines for everybody more than a half century ago. But countries need to flesh them out from time to time on the basis of their own recent experience.

The Bush administration has produced a radical overhaul of the U.S. manual. Given the Iraq experience, it is urgent that we reject this version and think again. We offer this book as a manageably sized, accessibly written, affordable compilation of key points that most urgently need to be rethought.

The idea of assembling lessons as tools for avoiding the next war is less of a stretch than it seems, given the group of writers represented here. These are people who know what they're talking about. They include a Nobel Prize–winning economist and his collaborator, whose analysis of the true costs of the war has become the most widely cited source on the topic. In these pages they have pushed their analysis wider and deeper than before. This much can be said: the next time a government official talks about a war paying for itself, as former deputy defense secretary Paul Wolfowitz did, that official won't get away with it. In Chapter 6, Joseph Stiglitz and Linda Bilmes have constructed the formula against which future debates over the costs of future wars will be judged.

Our writers also include the former chief UN weapons inspector, the world's principal prewar source for what turned out to be the truth about Iraqi weapons of mass destruction. If truth had been enough to stop a war, his work would have done it. And they include an Iraqi American whose weekly conversations with his relatives have given him a grim education in what living through a war to spread democracy is like on the ground. Also here is a Pulitzer Prize and National Book Award winner who traces the recurring American bad habit of starting wars as tryouts for big ideas. And we include one scholar who has earned his position of authority on wars for empire by sticking with the topic through three books, and another who has taken the same path to authority on wars for oil. To mention a few. We have asked them to boil down what they know for the rest of us.

These lessons are organized into three categories.

First come the "whys," the purposes that should never take us to war again. Iraq has been, foremost, a war of first resort. It was launched a year after our first national security doctrine of the new century replaced one based on avoiding war unless absolutely necessary, declaring that the old doctrine actually made war more likely. Wars had to be fought to prevent future enemies from developing. They would be fought to create the conditions for peace. For an analysis of this doctrine, read the first chapter in the collection; for an unnerving but exhilarating tour through the Orwellian minds of its adherents, read the last.

The Iraq war became the test bed for the ideological dream of delivering to the world a Pax Americana. It would spread the blessings of democracy while securing, by means of a dazzlingly superior military, the economic lifelines of oil and U.S.-favorable trade. This military would use the war to showcase its new weapons and its new ways of organizing itself and doing business with its allies.

The dream was hatched at least as far back as the end of the cold war, by those who saw their chance to solidify the position of the lone remaining superpower. The attacks of September 11, 2001, were seized, days or hours after they occurred, as the excuse to accelerate the engines of this goal to full power. As Defense Secretary Donald Rumsfeld said, Afghanistan lacked "good targets." So the idea became war with Iraq.

The book's second section focuses on the "hows," the ways and means that should never be allowed to take us into war again. The chapters in that section outline the administration's daring innovations in the manipulation of existing institutions: the United Nations and its international weapons inspectorate, U.S. intelligence agencies, major media. And their authors examine the companion piece to that effort, in the creation of false substitutes for these institutions: phony international coalitions, phony media, phony intelligence groups.

The last section surveys the major changes—what we call the "collateral damage"—to our national life and its constitutional foundation that have been achieved through war: the expansion of the power of the executive branch and the private sector and the constraint of our civil liberties. These achievements now have to be unachieved.

A word on what isn't here: These essays don't take part in the debate over how the war and ensuing occupation could have been done better. No question, they could have been. But this debate should not proceed unless it is tethered firmly to one fixed point, one inescapable conclusion, which is that this war should not have been fought at all. The reasons, enough of them, are here.

But assuredly not all of them. Our hope is that this list will spark reflections on what's missing and what's wrong. We hope that educators will lead exercises in prioritizing the list, disputing it, drawing connections among its items, discussing the extent to which these Iraq inventions are new or recycled. We hope there will be debate over whether and how these lessons, or others, could be turned into barricades marking the territory of these inventions out of bounds to future U.S. policymakers. We hope that citizens will take up these questions themselves. All of us have to try and finally make good on Senator McGovern's intent that "we'll never have to go down this road again."

Note

1. Dana Priest, "CIA Holds Terror Suspects in Secret Prisons," *Washington Post,* November 2, 2005; "Prewar CIA Report Doubted Claim That al Qaeda Sought WMD in Iraq," CNN.com, November 11, 2005; James Risen and Eric Lichtblau, "Bush Lets U.S. Spy on Callers Without Courts," *New York Times,* December 16, 2005.

Prologue

Anas Shallal

The people of England have been led in Mesopotamia [Iraq] into a trap from which it will be hard to escape with dignity and honour. They have been tricked into it by a steady withholding of information. The Baghdad communiqués are belated, insincere, incomplete. Things have been far worse than we have been told, our administration more bloody and inefficient than the public knows. It is a disgrace to our imperial record, and may soon be too inflamed for any ordinary cure. We are today not far from a disaster.

—*Published in the* Sunday Times, *August 22, 1920, by T. E. Lawrence*

On a cold Baghdad night in February 1963, an eight-year-old boy sat transfixed in front of the television as he watched the newly deposed Iraqi president, Abdul Karim Qassim, executed before a firing squad on Iraqi national television. The president sat on a folding chair with hands tied behind his back as he heard his sentence read. Then he was shot in the chest. Afterward, one executioner walked over to Qassim's limp body, grabbed his thick hair, yanked his head backward, and spit in his gaping mouth. The eight-year-old boy was me, and that image has haunted me for most of my life. Forty-four years later, I sat in front of a computer screen along with my fourteen-year-old daughter, watching a smuggled cell phone video of Saddam Hussein being taunted at the gallows, followed by the clank of the trap door opening from underneath his feet and the heavy rope swaying like a pendulum. We both sat in shock, unable to speak, as if we had just watched a snuff film.

The memory of that cold Baghdad night came rushing in. Iraq will have to brace itself for decades of continued bloodshed. How many more executions will Iraqis have to bear before they break this deadly cycle of hatred and revenge?

In 1958, Qassim's men had executed the prime minister of Iraq, Nouri al-Said. The body was dragged through the streets of Baghdad as throngs of citizens stood on either side watching it wither to bones behind a pickup truck.

They say if you don't learn from history, you are doomed to repeat it. And doomed we are. The proverbial sword is once again being wielded to rid Iraq of its memory. Perhaps it is a way to erase history and rewrite it. In the meantime, Iraqis are merely extras in a macabre theater of the absurd, with violence begetting more violence and setting the stage for the next blood-soaked moment.

Every new day in Iraq brings new horror stories. The two-year-old kidnapped and returned to his parents cooked on a platter. My fourteen-year-old nephew who was kidnapped for ransom and returned with scars from head to toe. Each story more horrific than the other. I have stopped asking relatives living there how things are because I know what the answer is going to be.

Recently, my aunt, who has lived in Baghdad through bad and worse—someone whose family had been persecuted by Saddam's regime; someone who lived through twelve years of sanctions—finally admitted that Baghdad has become, in her words, unlivable. "We cannot go out of the house; we cannot go to the market.... We have to send our young ones to the market because they don't have to worry about taking care of a family if, God forbid, they should get killed." She ended the conversation by quietly admitting, "I wish a missile will fall on our house and finish us once and for all.... I dread the sight of another day."

In the words of Nir Rosen of the New America Foundation, the Republic of Fear of Saddam Hussein has turned into "the democratic republic of fear." Freshly dug mass graves are uncovered routinely; men are being shot and killed for wearing shorts or having the wrong name; women cannot leave their homes without head-to-toe cover; mass arrests and collective punishment continue at an alarming rate. Death squads operate with impunity throughout Iraq, not only terrorizing neighborhoods but in many cases also running the prisons, acting as police, judge, and jury. According to the deputy minister of the interior, from Basra to Baghdad the prisons are out of government control, and the jails are infiltrated with militias from top to bottom.

The prison situation is so bad that in December 2005 the head of the American Detention Facilities, John Gardner, refused to turn over custody of the prisons to the Iraqi government, stating that such transfer would not occur until "The standards of inmate treatment and security match those maintained in U.S.-run facilities."[1]

In light of the conditions uncovered at U.S.-run prisons in Iraq, such as Abu Ghraib, it is baffling why such comments do not illicit massive outrage.

Since the invasion of Iraq, my aunt and her family have awakened every morning to yet another suicide bombing or explosion in the distance or the latest siege. Families have to scurry to get home at night for fear of marauding gangs. Most of my cousins and their friends have left the country and have become refugees in nearby Arab countries. Unemployment averages 40 to 70 percent, according to the Ministry of Labor. Electricity and water are scarce. "Three hours of electricity is a good day," my aunt told me recently. The sight and smell of rotting human flesh has become commonplace. A bloated body lying in the street has become normal, ignored or stepped over as Iraqis go about their daily chores. Their ears have become numb to the sound of bombs and screams.

There is not an Iraqi left who has not witnessed violent death first-hand.

"You can keep your democracy," my aunt told me, referring to George W. Bush's assertion that we are spreading democracy in Iraq. Iraqis are far less concerned about democracy than about their basic human needs: food, shelter, and safety for themselves and their families.

In early 2006, an Iraqi National Assembly committee, made up of Shiite and Kurdish legislators, concluded that the only way Iraq could achieve sovereignty was for multinational forces to leave. Their report called for setting a timetable for the troops to go home and referred to them as "occupation forces," a first.[2]

The United States and its coalition of the dwindling entered Iraq using Mapquest and a tourist map—they were led to believe by a few café elites living in posh quarters in London and Washington that the invasion would be a cakewalk, that flowers and sweets would rain upon their arrival.

As we continue to stay the course, or worse, do more of the same, more innocent people are caught in the crossfire. The rhetoric of reconciliation and rebuilding is buried beneath the rubble of homes and the dust that never seems to settle. Tears are soon turned to anger and hatred, providing the oxygen for a fierce and relentless resistance that is growing and spreading from Basra to Mosul, from Khaniqeen to Tal Afar to Baghdad.

The paint-by-numbers government that was ushered in by the United States and its allies has all the makings of a setup for a continued civil war. This, combined with outside intervention by neighboring countries such as Iran and others, has created a cauldron for future internal and regional conflicts.

It must be clear by now that war was not the way to bring democracy to Iraq. Each violent transfer of power in Iraq has brought more hatred and further violence. Iraq's cycle of violent political change must be broken, not perpetuated.

Five years after this war began, Iraq is on the verge of being a failed state. The Iraqi parliament is for the most part dysfunctional and out of touch with the needs of the Iraqi people. Ordinary Iraqis see little improvement in their day-to-day lives and have seen worsening conditions under this elected body. The promised democracy that this invasion was going to spread has all but vanished, overshadowed by lawlessness and unimaginable violence. Iraq has become "the best recruiting tool"[3] for terrorists. It is hard to imagine that some of the most ardent advocates of this war have been privately whispering that things were better under Saddam's regime. "At least we had electricity and could walk safely to the market," a friend told me.

What does that say about the future of Iraq? Is this an opening for another strongman to "save" Iraq? Many Iraqis have been advocating for such a scenario, opening the path for the next Saddam Hussein or worse.

As for the region, this war has provided much-needed cover for fundamentalists in Iran and other neighboring countries. Real democratic reforms have been set back decades. A crackdown on dissent is seen as essential to national security.

Each day that this war continues, U.S. standing in the world community is diminished. As a naturalized American, I feel a strong sense of duty to make sure that this country continues to stand for the values that brought my family and millions of others to its shores—the values of freedom and liberty, the values of government of, by, and for the people. I am outraged when I see such values trampled upon by the very people whom we elect to uphold them. After all, isn't the chief role of government to uphold those values?

I am outraged when my government engages in a war that is immoral and illegal.

I am outraged when my government detains people without any charges and holds them indefinitely.

I am outraged when my government shackles and secretly transports people all over the globe to be imprisoned and tortured in secret prisons outside international law.

I am outraged when my government eavesdrops on my phone conversations.

I am outraged when my government engages in torture and war crimes.

How is it that my government threatens Iran with sanctions and even a military attack because of a nuclear program, while allowing Israel to possess between 100 and 400 nuclear weapons without even a whimper?

In a time when the Geneva Conventions are being called "quaint" by our top officials and preventive war has become acceptable, we have to take these threats seriously.

I want my government to lead by the strength of its convictions and values—not by the size of its weapons. Surely the former is a far more lasting legacy for future generations.

Many Iraqis I speak to believe that what is going on right now in Iraq is temporary and will lead to a brighter future, that this is just the untidy cost of freedom. I believe that you cannot have a peaceful future by claiming a moral high ground while acting immorally. When the ends continue to justify the means, we risk becoming the very evil we are fighting against.

As I remember the moment that I stared at the television, watching Qassim's execution, I see that not very much has changed in the last forty-four years. I wonder how many more executions my fourteen-year-old daughter will witness, how much more bloodshed will have to be shed in the name of justice. I remember my aunt and wonder whether I will ever be able to see her again.

Notes

1. Eric Schmitt and Thom Shanker, "U.S., Citing Abuse in Iraqi Prisons, Holds Detainees," *New York Times,* December 25, 2005.

2. Iraq National Sovereignty Committee Report, September 16, 2005.

3. Brian Wheeler, BBC, October 20, 2005.

Purposes

Chapter 1

The Dangerous Leap

Preventive War

Neta C. Crawford

Preventive war advocates apparently have common sense on their side. In the sixteenth century Italian international law scholar Alberico Gentili said, "No one ought to expose himself to danger. No one ought to wait to be struck, unless he is a fool.... One ought to provide not only against an offence which is being committed, but also against one which may possibly be committed. Force must be repelled and kept aloof by force. Therefore one should not wait for it to come."

In 1757 Benjamin Franklin traveled to London to urge that Britain ensure its security in North America by expelling the French from Canada. British pamphleteer William Burke argued against the idea: "to desire the enemy's whole country on no other principle but that otherwise you cannot secure your own, is turning the idea of mere defense into the most dangerous of all principles. . . . It is leaving no medium between safety and conquest. It is to suppose yourself never safe, whilst your neighbor enjoys security."[1]

Supposing itself never safe, the Bush administration has claimed a right of preemption, arguing that "new technology requires new thinking about when a threat actually becomes 'imminent.' So as a matter of common sense, the United States must be prepared to take action, when necessary, before threats have fully materialized."[2] They claim that the "best defense is a good offense."[3]

Yet their policy is not simply preemption. Preemptive action may legitimately be undertaken when a state faces an *immediate* (imminent) and *credible* threat from an aggressor and seeks to eliminate the threat before it can be grievously harmed. Preemptors believe that they act in self-defense—that aggressive action by an adversary is inevitable, that the attack is about to occur, that they can find the other's threatening military assets, and that a preemptive strike can eliminate or dramatically reduce the imminent threat.

The Bush administration conflates and confuses preemptive war with preventive war. In defending their new doctrine of prevention, Condoleezza Rice once referred to Daniel Webster's "very famous defense of anticipatory self-defense."[4] In fact, Webster's argument about a British attack on an American ship clarifies why prevention must not be mistaken for preemption.

In December 1837 British military forces based in Canada learned that a private American ship, the *Caroline,* was ferrying arms, recruits, and supplies from Buffalo, New York, to a group of anti-British rebels on the Canadian side of the border. On the night of December 29, British and Canadian forces set out to destroy the ship. They eventually found the ship berthed in U.S. waters. While most of the *Caroline's* crew slept, the troops boarded the ship, attacked the crew and passengers, and set the ship on fire. The events nearly led to war between the United States and Britain when U.S. citizens mobilized to respond. Diplomatic correspondence over the incident continued for years. British ambassador Henry Fox defended the incursion into U.S. territory and the raid on the *Caroline,* arguing that British forces were simply acting in self-defense, protecting themselves against "unprovoked attack" with preemptive force.[5]

Secretary of State Daniel Webster responded by articulating a set of criteria for acting with a "necessity of self-defense"—in particular for a legitimate use of preemptive force—that has become the touchstone of international law on this question. Preemption, Webster argued, is justified only in response to an *imminent* threat and must be limited to responding to that threat. Webster argued that the British attack failed miserably by these standards: "It will be for that Government to show a necessity of self-defence, instant, overwhelming, leaving no choice of means, and no moment for deliberation."

> the act, justified by the necessity of self-defense, must be limited by that necessity, and kept clearly within it. It must be shown that ... daylight could not be waited for; that there could be no attempt at discrimination between the innocent and the guilty; that it would not have been enough to seize and detain the vessel; but that there was a necessity, present and inevitable, for attacking her in the darkness of night, ... while unarmed men were asleep on board, killing some and wound[ing] others, and then ... setting her on fire, and, careless to know whether there might not be in her the innocent with the guilty, or the living with the dead, committing her to a fate which fills the imagination with horror. A necessity for all this the government of the United States cannot believe to have existed.

Webster concludes, "if such things [as the attack on the *Caroline*] be allowed to occur, they must lead to bloody and exasperated war."[6]

The attack on the *Caroline* was not preemptive but preventive. A preventive war or strike is undertaken when a state believes that war with a potential adversary is likely in the indefinite future and that waiting will cause the loss of military advantage. The threat is not imminent or even certain to materialize in the near future. The preventive attacker assumes a worst-case scenario—that the potential adversary will, one day, certainly attack, and that no negotiation, change in circumstance, or alteration in the adversary's goals could intervene.[7]

The United States launched a preventive war against Iraq in March 2003, arguing that Iraq's weapons of mass destruction and its government's hostility to the United States posed a "grave and gathering" threat. Other administration arguments—that Saddam Hussein was a tyrant, that Iraq might soon support al-Qaeda if it had not done so already, and that democratization of Iraq by force would lead to democratization of the Middle East—varied in prominence. The key claim, however, was that Iraq's drive for military power, combined with its history of regional aggression, would one day make Iraq a threat to the United States.

Assuming, for the sake of argument, that the Bush administration's assessment of Iraq's weapons of mass destruction resulted from genuine error rather than deliberate deception, preventive war was the wrong policy. As Webster argues, preemption might sometimes be wise and necessary. Preventive war is always dangerous; although it might make intuitive sense to stamp out all potential future threats and it is sometimes prudent to engage in preemption, preventive war makes the United States less secure. If, as Gentili said, only a "fool" would wait to be struck if they can see the blow coming, it is worse to announce a policy of starting wars against potential future adversaries.

Flawed Logic

The Bush administration makes two dangerous leaps in logic. First, it distorts the idea of *self*-defense by defining the U.S. "self" in increasingly broad terms, going beyond simply defending U.S. borders and citizens. The administration includes among the "enduring national interests" of the United States to be secured by force those that "contribut[e] to economic well-being," which include the "vitality and productivity of the global economy" and "access to key markets and strategic resources."[8] The declared goal of U.S. strategy is to maintain "preeminence." "America has, and intends to keep, military strengths beyond challenge...."[9] And, perhaps most strikingly, the administration claims, "Today the distinction between domestic and foreign affairs is diminishing."[10]

When U.S. interests and assets are defined as *global*, no region or issue is potentially beyond immediate U.S. concern and in need of control. Therefore President Bush argues, "Our security will require ... a military that must be ready to strike at a moment's notice in any dark corner of the world. And our security will require all Americans to be forward-looking and resolute, to be ready for preemptive action when necessary to defend our liberty and to defend our lives."[11] Leaving no medium between safety and conquest, the U.S. self thus becomes an imperial self and, in this view, the United States must be prepared to intervene everywhere at any time.

If the self is defined so broadly and threats to this greater "self" are met with military force, at what point does self-defense begin to look, at least to outside observers, like aggression? As Richard Betts argues, "When security is defined in terms broader than protecting the near-term integrity of national sovereignty and borders, the distinction between offense and defense blurs hopelessly ... security can be as insatiable an appetite as acquisitiveness—there may never be enough buffers."[12]

Second, the Bush administration collapses distinctions between major and minor threats and imminent and distant threats, exaggerating the dangers that its opponents pose. Even if terrorists cannot be deterred, their capacities are limited. Though any loss of life is tragic, the administration conflates those threats that pose a grave danger to the existence of the United States and those that might hurt some number of people.

A U.S.-Soviet nuclear war involving tens of thousands of nuclear weapons during the cold war was a much greater threat than that posed today by terrorists—even those armed with some number of weapons of mass destruction—yet successive U.S. administrations rejected preventive war against the Soviets as too dangerous.[13] Further, the administration erases the distinction between present or imminent threats and possible future threat. An imminent threat is one in which the blow is on the way. But the administration assumes that even distant threats are lethal and that nothing can stop them. If the administration is right that we will not see a terrorist strike before it arrives, then primary prevention through diplomacy, arms control, and the alleviation of the grievances that give rise to terrorism is the best hope for reducing the likelihood of a terrorist strike.

If the distinctions between major and minor threats and imminent and possible future threats are not used to assess the security situation, then preventive war, or the threat of it, becomes the strategy of first resort.

The Dangers of Preventive War

The urge to prevent war is rooted in understandable impulses—the desire to banish all fear and uncertainty about threats and the desire for imperial control, itself ultimately also rooted in both fear and hubris. If preventive war could guarantee security from future attack or permanent preeminence, it might indeed be the policy of choice. But the psychological reassurance promised by preventive offensive war doctrines is illusory at best, and at worst, preventive war is a recipe for conflict and risk. Fear can never be banished, and total security through total control is impossible. Preventive war doctrines and preventive wars are dangerous even for states with imperial aspirations.

First, preventive war doctrines militarize disputes that might otherwise be resolved without the threat or use of military force. Unlike preemption, which is the reaction to an immediate and grave threat, preventive force is undertaken with a long time horizon. But even if the other is intent on aggression at some point, the situation may be open to change. War might not be inevitable. As Otto von Bismarck said to Wilhelm I in 1875, "I would ... never advise Your Majesty to declare war forthwith, simply because it appeared that our opponent would begin hostilities in the near future. One can never anticipate the ways of divine providence securely enough for that."[14]

Second, the threat and use of preventive force heightens international insecurity. When one state declares a preventive war doctrine, potential and actual adversaries may, justifiably, feel threatened and begin mobilizing for war. Preventive doctrines may thus promote a spiral of anticipation. When threatened states arm against a promised attack, the pressures to conduct a preventive war increase. War becomes a self-fulfilling prophesy.

Third, actual preventive war is dangerous in both the short and long term because any preventive use of military force entails all the risks of war. To undertake war at any time is to open oneself to risk. Any war can go terribly wrong. The promised quick and surgical intervention may degenerate into a long-term bloodbath. Neighbors may intervene, and war may escalate. And preventive war potentially entails the loss of one's own soldiers in an optional conflict.

Fourth, these risks to the self are potentially increased by the harm to the target of preventive war. Those states that are seen to exercise an imperial prerogative always breed resentment and resistance. Because a state begins a preventive war before the other side has used force, or even mobilized against it, by definition the aggressor state has not been acted upon militarily. Therefore, even if they might one day have become soldiers, most, if not all, of those injured by the preventive war are noncombatants. Preventive war thus violates the just war and international law prohibition against harming noncombatants. The fellow citizens of the innocents killed and maimed by preventive wars will understandably resent those who started the war. Further, the use of preventive force says that the aspirations, grievances, and conduct of the target of preventive war are illegitimate. Those aspirations and the means the state might use to pursue them may or may not turn out to be legitimate, but to wage war preventively assumes that the other's aspirations can never be justified. Their hopes will remain frustrated, and the chance for peaceful resolution of any disputes has been forfeited. It is precisely this sense of grievance that terrorists use in their recruitment and mobilization efforts.

Well before his trip to London, Benjamin Franklin famously said that "an ounce of prevention is worth a pound of cure." But preventive doctrines and preventive war offer only illusory preventive effects and no real protection. Rather, preventive war vitiates the opportunities for real prevention offered by economic and cultural exchange, arms control, and diplomacy.

Notes

I thank Alice Whitehill Wiseberg for her thoughtful comments.

1. Gentili, quoted in Richard Tuck, *The Rights of War and Peace: Political Thought and the International Order from Grotius to Kant* (Oxford: Oxford University

Press, 1999), p. 18. Burke, quoted in Walter LeFeber, *The American Age: U.S. Foreign Policy at Home and Abroad,* Vol. 1: *To 1920* (New York: W. W. Norton, 1994) pp. 14–15.

2. Condoleezza Rice, October 1, 2002, to the Manhattan Institute, New York, New York.

3. *The National Security Strategy of the United States of America* (Washington, DC: Office of the President, September 2002), p. 6; *National Strategy for Combating Terrorism* (Washington, DC: White House, 2003), p. 24.

4. Rice, quoted in David E. Sanger, "Beating Them to the Prewar," *New York Times,* September 28, 2002, p. B7.

5. Fox, letter to Daniel Webster, March 12, 1841, in Kenneth E. Shewmaker, ed., *The Papers of Daniel Webster: Diplomatic Papers,* Vol. 1: *1841–1843* (Hanover, NH: University Press of New England, 1983), p. 42.

6. Webster, letter to Fox, April 24, 1841, in Shewmaker, ed., *The Papers of Daniel Webster,* pp. 62, 67–68.

7. Preventive war is not true prevention of violent conflict through diplomatic or other nonmilitary means.

8. Department of Defense, *Quadrennial Defense Review* (Washington, DC: U.S. Government Printing Office, September 30, 2001), p. 2.

9. Ibid., pp. 30 and 62; and George W. Bush remarks at June 1, 2002, Graduation Exercise of the U.S. Military Academy, West Point, New York. Transcript, www.whitehouse.gov/news/releases/2002.

10. *National Security Strategy,* p. 31.

11. Remarks by Bush, West Point, June 1, 2002.

12. Richard K. Betts, *Surprise Attack* (Washington, DC: Brookings Institution, 1982), pp. 142, 143.

13. Marc Tractenberg, "Preventive War and U.S. Foreign Policy," in Henry Shue and David Rodin, eds., *Preemption: Military Action and Moral Justification* (Oxford: Oxford University Press, 2007).

14. Quoted in Gordon A. Craig, *The Politics of the Prussian Army, 1640–1945* (Oxford: Oxford University Press, 1955), p. 255.

Chapter 2

American Imperialism

Enabler of War

Chalmers Johnson

Ira Chernus, author of *Monsters to Destroy: The Neoconservative War on Terror and Sin,* warns us that now that the "surge" in Baghdad has proven to be an utter failure, the ground has been prepared in Washington to explain the Iraq disaster as a self-inflicted wound. The conventional narrative will suggest that "we" were denied "victory" by a combination of a vacillating public, a treasonous Democratic Congress, and a lack of sufficient will to dominate the world. As Chernus writes, "We'll be told that Iraq, too, was just an aberration, a well-intentioned war handled with a staggering level of incompetence that simply got out of control. Those who don't want to repeat the experience, who prefer to try other paths to global security, will be told they are infected with the Iraq syndrome. And the prescription for a cure will inevitably be military buildup, imperial war, and, of course, the possibility of ... 'kicking' the Iraq syndrome."[1]

I believe that the U.S. commitment to empire after the cold war foreordained the outcome in Iraq. Americans concluded that they had "won" the cold war, had become a new Rome, were now the "lone superpower" enjoying "full spectrum dominance" over the planet, and should employ preventive wars of choice to ensure that no combination of friends or enemies could ever challenge us militarily. Those assumptions about the U.S. role in the world sealed its fate, and serious mistakes like Iraq became inevitable.

The Iraq debacle could have been prevented if the constitutional system of checks and balances had been intact and functioning in the United States. But constitutionally mandated restraints had been replaced by the most secretive "imperial presidency" in U.S. history, while the president himself went about insisting, "I am the decider."[2]

History tells us that one of the most unstable political combinations is a country, like the United States today, that tries to be both a domestic democracy and a foreign imperialist. The impacts of the Iraq war—at home and abroad—bear out this point. The U.S. attempt to combine domestic democracy with tyranny over foreigners is hopelessly contradictory and hypocritical. A country can be democratic, or it can be imperialist, but it cannot for long be both. The U.S. political system failed to prevent this combination from developing, and I believe that it is by now probably incapable of correcting it. The evidence strongly suggests the legislative and judicial branches of the U.S. government have become so servile in the presence of the imperial presidency that they have largely lost the ability to respond in a principled and independent manner.

Some people question whether what the United States does abroad as a nation can be called imperialism. The British ruled India, much of Africa, and large swaths of the Middle East through their colonies. They did not seek consent; they dominated these places through direct military force. Imperialism never seeks consent; it is a pure form of tyranny. Similarly, the Dutch reigned over Indonesia, the French over Indochina and Algeria, and the Japanese over Korea and Taiwan. Those, too, we recognize as empires. But what the Russians had in Eastern Europe—the system of satellites from Bulgaria to East Germany, ruled through the Soviet Red Army—was also a form of empire. Moscow dominated these countries through huge military forces stationed on their borders or based in their territories, local pro-Soviet puppets, and economic integration into the Soviet-bloc system.

A dominant power with satellites, not colonies, is the sort of empire the United States has created and is now trying to maintain—by way of its military forces and its bases, and threats such as those it issues routinely against Iran, North Korea, Venezuela, the Palestinians, and other regimes we don't approve of. Over half a million U.S. troops, spies, contractors, dependents, and others are now stationed on some 737 military bases located in more than 130 countries, according to official Pentagon inventories. Many of these foreign countries are presided over by dictatorial regimes that have given their citizens no say in the decision to let the United States in. To run this empire, the president relies mostly on the Pentagon and the Central Intelligence Agency (CIA) and has assumed powers specifically denied him by the Constitution. A Republican-dominated Congress simply abdicated its responsibilities to balance the power of the executive branch; despite the Democratic sweep in the 2006 election, it remains to be seen whether these tendencies can be reversed or controlled.

Specifically, I believe that maintaining that empire abroad requires resources and commitments that will inevitably undercut U.S. domestic democracy and could, in the end, produce a military dictatorship or its civilian equivalent. The combination of huge standing armies, almost continuous wars, the growing domestic economic dependence on the military-industrial complex, and ruinous military expenses are destroying the U.S. republican structure in favor of an imperial presidency. By republican structure, I mean, of course, the separation of powers and elaborate checks and balances that the founders of the United States wrote into the Constitution as the main bulwarks against tyranny.

Americans are in danger of losing their democracy for the sake of keeping their empire. Once a nation starts down that path, the dynamics that apply to all empires come into play—isolation, overstretch, the uniting of forces opposed to imperialism, and bankruptcy. The Iraq war is the latest signpost on this road to ruin.

History is instructive on this dilemma. If Americans choose to keep the empire, as the Romans did, they will certainly lose their democracy and grimly await the eventual blowback that imperialism generates.

There is an alternative, however. The United States could, like the British Empire after World War II, keep its democracy by giving up its empire. The British did not do a particularly brilliant job of liquidating their empire, and there were several clear cases in which British imperialists defied their nation's commitment to democracy in order to keep their foreign privileges. Kenya in the 1950s and the Anglo-French-Israeli invasion of Egypt in 1956 are particularly savage examples. But the overall thrust of postwar

British history in light of the allied defeat of Nazism is clear: The people of the British Isles chose democracy over imperialism.

In her book *The Origins of Totalitarianism,* the political philosopher Hannah Arendt writes about British imperialism:

> On the whole it was a failure because of the dichotomy between the nation-state's legal principles and the methods needed to oppress other people permanently. This failure was neither necessary nor due to ignorance or incompetence. British imperialists knew very well that "administrative massacres" could keep India in bondage, but they also knew that public opinion at home would not stand for such measures. Imperialism could have been a success if the nation-state had been willing to pay the price, to commit suicide and transform itself into a tyranny. It is one of the glories of Europe, and especially of Great Britain, that she preferred to liquidate the empire.[3]

I agree with this judgment. When one looks at the Blair government's unnecessary and futile support of Bush's invasion of Iraq, one can only conclude that it was an atavistic response, a British longing to relive the glories—and cruelties—of their past.

Could the American people themselves restore constitutional government? A grassroots movement to abolish the CIA, break the hold of the military-industrial complex, and establish public financing of elections may be possible. But given corporate control of the mass media and the difficulties of mobilizing a large and diverse population, it seems unlikely. If the costs and consequences of the Iraq war and the pervasive assault on civil liberties carried out since September 11 are not sufficient to generate a mass democratic uprising, it is not clear what will be.

It is possible that, at some future moment, the U.S. military could actually take over the government and declare a dictatorship (though they undoubtedly would find a gentler, more user-friendly name for it). That is, after all, how the Roman republic ended, by being turned over to a populist general, Julius Caesar, who after his assassination was succeeded by his grand-nephew, Octavian, who then proclaimed himself dictator for life and named himself Emperor Augustus Caesar.

I think it unlikely that the U.S. military will go that route. But one cannot ignore the fact that professional military officers played a considerable role in getting rid of their civilian overlord, Donald Rumsfeld. His replacement, Robert Gates, comes from the super-secretive CIA, and might be receptive to an unconstitutional scheme hatched by rogue military officers.

Meanwhile, the all-volunteer army has become an ever-more-separate institution in American society, its profile less and less like that of the general populace. As the wars in both Iraq and Afghanistan drag on and the failure to "win" becomes evident to one and all, the bitterness of the professional troops will increase. The failure of the government to lavish care and pensions on its seriously wounded veterans and their families is also likely to fester.[4]

Nonetheless, the officer corps might well worry about how the American people would react to a move toward open military dictatorship. Moreover, prosecutions of low-level military torturers from Abu Ghraib prison and killers of civilians in Iraq have demonstrated to enlisted ranks that obedience to illegal orders can result in their being punished, whereas officers go free. No one knows whether ordinary American soldiers would obey clearly illegal orders to oust an elected government or whether the officer corps has sufficient confidence to issue such orders.

The present system already offers the military high command so much—in funds, prestige, and future employment via the military–industrial revolving door—that a perilous transition to anything like direct military rule would make little sense under reasonably normal conditions.

So my guess is that the United States will maintain a façade of constitutional government and drift along until financial bankruptcy overtakes it. The full costs of the Iraq war—estimated at up to $2 trillion—will be an important contributing factor to this looming fiscal insolvency.

Of course, bankruptcy will not mean the literal end of the United States any more than it did for Germany in 1923, China in 1948, or Argentina in 2001–2002. It might, in fact, open the way for an unexpected restoration of the U.S. system, for military rule, for revolution, or simply for some new development we cannot yet imagine. Certainly, such a bankruptcy would mean a drastic lowering of the U.S. standard of living; a loss of control over international affairs; a process of adjusting to the rise of other powers, including China and India; and a further discrediting of the notion that the United States is somehow exceptional compared to other nations.

Americans would have to learn what it means to be a far poorer nation and the attitudes and manners that go with it. As Anatol Lieven, author of *America Right or Wrong: An Anatomy of American Nationalism,* concludes, "U.S. global power, as presently conceived by the overwhelming majority of the U.S. establishment, is unsustainable.... The empire can no longer raise enough taxes or soldiers, it is increasingly indebted, and key vassal states are no longer reliable.... The result is that the empire can no longer pay for enough of the professional troops it needs to fulfill its self-assumed imperial tasks."[5]

So I believe (and hope) that the U.S. imperial venture will end not with a nuclear bang but a financial whimper. It seems to me unlikely that a president (or Congress) from either party will manage to dismantle the military-industrial complex, end the secrecy and the "black budgets" that make public oversight of what the government does impossible, and bring the president's secret army, the CIA, under democratic control. In order to prevent future Iraqs, Americans need to abandon at least 700 of their 737 overseas bases, along with the imperial hubris that helps set the stage for such ill-conceived military misadventures. If they don't do so, the issue is likely to become moot as a result of internal fiscal collapse.

Notes

1. Ira Chernus, "Will We Suffer from the Iraq Syndrome?" TomDispatch, March 1, 2007, http://www.tomdispatch.com/index.mhtml?pid=170608.

2. "Bush: 'I'm the Decider' on Rumsfeld," CNN, April 18, 2006, http://www.cnn.com/2006/POLITICS/04/18/rumsfeld/.

3. Hannah Arendt, *The Origins of Totalitarianism* (New York: Meridian, 1958), pp. 503–504.

4. See, e.g., David S. Cloud, "Army Secretary Ousted in Furor on Hospital Care," *New York Times,* March 3, 2007.

5. Anatol Lieven, "Decadent America Must Give Up Imperial Ambitions," *Financial Times,* November 29, 2005.

Chapter 3

Ideas Floating Free

War as Demonstration Model

Frances FitzGerald

Bush's decision to invade Iraq alarmed many who had served in the Vietnam War or who had reported on it as journalists, and later we found our worst fears confirmed: U.S. officials had once again sent American soldiers to fight a guerrilla war without the support of the population, or even of the government they helped install. Further, they had once again chosen to go to war unilaterally and against a regime that had in no way threatened the vital national security interests of the United States. How could this happen again, we asked each other?

Iraq is, of course, not Vietnam. The two countries could hardly be less alike; and although many more lives were lost in Vietnam than have been in Iraq so far, this unprovoked war will have consequences for the United

States and the world that Vietnam never had. Still, in both cases, the decision to invade rested on a set of assumptions divorced from the reality on the ground. Examining these assumptions is not just a matter of historical interest, for ideas have a life of their own, and some survive even the most brutal clashes with reality.[1]

U.S. presidents have in the past made costly mistakes based on faulty intelligence or misreading of the data. (John F. Kennedy's decision to authorize the invasion of Cuba at the Bay of Pigs is a good example.) But the commitment of American troops to Vietnam was not one of them, and no more was Bush's decision to invade Iraq. If not Bush himself, then Vice President Richard Cheney, Secretary of Defense Donald Rumsfeld, and the others who drove the war policy forward knew in 2002 that the available intelligence did not show that Saddam Hussein had weapons of mass destruction or ties to al-Qaeda. They simply presumed he had both, and lacking any hard evidence, they created small teams, one in the vice president's office and the other in the Defense Department, to pick out factoids from the raw intelligence data that would bolster their case and advertised them as fact.

Then, too, when asked about the future of Iraq, Bush spoke of democracy and freedom, unburdened by any information about the history of the country or the constituents of its society. In January 2003, he was, according to two pro-invasion Iraqi Americans who met with him, unfamiliar with the terms *Sunni* and *Shiite.* Apparently no one in the White House had thought it important to brief the president on the two major sects in Islam. But then, the other architects of the invasion were equally incurious about Iraq and its fraught history of ethnic and sectarian conflict. They had simply made up their minds that Saddam Hussein was responsible for all the problems in Iraq and that removing him would solve them. They refused to take any counsel about what was not known and what could not be predicted.

The architects of the war—Bush, Cheney, Rumsfeld, Wolfowitz, and others—were in the grip of a vision, or a series of interlocking visions, that had little to do with Iraq itself. In 1990, just after the fall of the Berlin Wall, Cheney, then secretary of defense in George H. W. Bush's administration, created an interagency group to articulate the political and military mission of the United States in the post–cold war world. The group, which included Wolfowitz, then deputy secretary of defense for policy, Cheney's aide Lewis Libby, and Zalmay Khalilzad, then on the National Security Council (NSC) staff, delivered its recommendations in February 1992 as a draft of the annual Defense Planning Guidance. The draft, leaked to the *New York Times,* asserted that the U.S. mission was to ensure that no rival emerged in any part of the world. The United States, the document stated, "must maintain the mechanism for deterring potential competitors from even aspiring to a larger regional or global role." It described Russia and China as potential threats and warned that Germany, Japan, and other industrial powers might be tempted to rearm and acquire nuclear weapons if their security was threatened. The authors of the document therefore recommended that the Pentagon take measures, including, if necessary, the use of force, to prevent the proliferation of weapons of mass destruction in such countries such as North Korea and Iraq. The document made no mention of collective action through the United Nations, and while acknowledging that military coalitions could be useful, it maintained that "we should expect future coalitions to be ad hoc assemblies, often not lasting beyond the crisis to be confronted."[2]

The document did not mesh with the views of Bush 41, and after some controversy, the draft was withdrawn and replaced. But it did represent the emerging views of hard-line nationalists, such as Cheney, and of neoconservatives, such as Wolfowitz, and with the election of George W. Bush in 2000, this vision became the basis for the foreign policy of the United States.

In its first seven months the Bush administration paid far less attention to the threat of al-Qaeda than to "regime change" in Iraq. While officials went about extricating the United States from a series of treaties limiting weapons of mass destruction, the Defense and State Departments circulated dozens of reports on a possible invasion of Iraq. In the view of many in the administration, the overthrow of Saddam Hussein would serve two purposes. First, it would eliminate one rogue state with nuclear ambitions and deter the rest by sending a powerful message about U.S. power and resolve. Second, it would change the balance of forces in the Middle East.

The scenario publicly articulated by administration officials and echoed by pundits of all sorts in 2002–2003 was that the regime that would replace Saddam Hussein's would demonstrate the wonders of freedom and democracy and cause a tsunami of democratic reforms in the Middle East, bringing down the mullahs in Tehran, the Baathists in Syria, and Arab autocrats elsewhere. The analogies officials used were to Germany and Japan after World War II and Eastern Europe after the end of the cold war. Of course, not all administration officials shared this particular dream. For others, like Cheney and Rumsfeld, who fancied themselves as hardheaded realists, the vision of cascading democracies served more as an attractive cover for U.S. interests. The overthrow of Hussein by a lightning strike on Baghdad would "shock and awe" the states in the region. It would show the regimes in Syria and Iran that they had to change their behavior or risk the

same fate, and it would persuade other Arab rulers that they should cooperate more closely with the United States. Then, with their state sponsors
gone, Hamas, Hezbollah, and Palestine Liberation Organization (PLO)
chairman Yasir Arafat would fade from the scene, and Israel could make the
peace it wanted with the Palestinians. Further, Iraq with a friendly, secular
regime would provide a new source of oil and lessen U.S. dependence on
the Saudi monarchy; in addition, it would harbor U.S. military bases and
help to extend a Pax Americana across the region.

In the wake of the attacks on September 11, 2001, Bush and his officials
might have decided to change their focus and build international support for a
long-term campaign against al-Qaeda. Instead, they immediately found new
reasons to invade Iraq. One of their reasons, according to Richard Clarke, the
senior advisor to the National Security Council (NSC) on counterterrorism,
was "a felt need to do something big" to respond to 9/11, "a fast, bold, simple
move that would send a signal at home and abroad that said, 'don't mess with
Texas or America.'" Another, according to those attending NSC meetings
in this period, was "to create a demonstration model to guide the behavior of
anyone with the temerity to acquire destructive weapons or, in any way, flout
the authority of the United States." Yet another, according to Douglas Feith,
deputy secretary of defense for policy, was that U.S. military action against
Iraq "would register with other countries around the world that are sponsor-
ing terrorism, and would perhaps change their cost-benefit calculation."

That Saddam Hussein had nothing to do with the 9/11 attacks or with
al-Qaeda was beside the point for these strategists. Asked by Bush's chief
speech writer, Michael Gerson, why he supported the war, Henry Kissinger
replied, "Because Afghanistan wasn't enough." In the conflict with radical
Islam, he said, they want to humiliate us. "And we need to humiliate them."
Much the same kind of thinking was going on inside the administration. In
a campaign speech in 2004, Condoleezza Rice explained, "While Saddam
Hussein had nothing to do with the actual attacks on America, Saddam's
Iraq was a part of the Middle East that was festering and unstable [and]
was a part of the circumstances that created the problem in 2001." The
United States could not attack Egypt or Saudi Arabia, where most of the
9/11 terrorists came from, and, unlike Iran, Iraq was thought to be an easy
target. So, Saddam Hussein's secular regime was to stand in for all radical
Islamists, all terrorists, and the states that sponsored them.

That, in sum, was the fantasy world that Bush, Cheney, Rumsfeld, Rice,
and the other architects of the war had created for themselves. A Hobbesian
world of competing nation-states, where nuclear weapons and conventional
military forces were the sole determinants of power; a world where the
United States, unfettered by treaties, international law, or commitments

to allies, could attack any country at will and where this demonstration of power and resolve would cause all other governments to fall in behind it—or topple one after another. It was a world of abstractions—such as "democracy" and "terrorism"—that floated free of any particular place or set of persons, a world invented in Washington by ideologues and polemicists.

This fantasy world was unique to the Bush administration, but it had an intellectual history in a strain of thinking that ran through the Republican Midwest from the second half of the nineteenth century until World War II. In this period, men from William McKinley to Robert A. Taft counseled a foreign policy that amounted to isolationism vis-à-vis Europe and imperialism vis-à-vis the Caribbean and the Far East. This foreign policy, which the historian Charles Beard identified as "imperial isolationism"—as opposed to the "collective internationalism" of Republicans and Democrats on the East Coast—came from a particular imagination of the world. Looking across the Atlantic, Midwesterners saw an Old World that was decadent, feudal, and corrupt, its teeming masses a cauldron of radical ideas and its politicians endlessly intriguing to embroil the United States in ancient, incomprehensible quarrels. To the south and the west, however, lay countries inhabited by peoples of alien cultures that were technologically and militarily inferior to the United States. To most Midwesterners these countries were pure abstractions, mere objects of national pride, commercial activity, and the American civilizing mission. "With God's help, we will lift Shanghai up and up until it is just like Kansas City," Senator Keith Wherry of Nebraska, one of Taft's closest allies, declared. Under the circumstances, Midwesterners saw no need for alliances or for diplomacy. "It is the pattern of Oriental psychology to respect and follow aggressive, dynamic and resolute leadership," General Douglas MacArthur averred. It was the Republican heirs to this tradition who in the 1950s and early 1960s claimed that the United States had "lost China" and proposed to "roll back" Soviet power in Eastern Europe with nuclear weapons, if necessary.

Lyndon Johnson did not belong to this tradition, but along with a policy of intervention in Vietnam, he inherited the driving force behind it: the idea that if South Vietnam "fell to communism," then the rest of the Southeast Asian countries from the Chinese border on down—Laos, Cambodia, Thailand, Indonesia, and the Philippines—would fall to communism like so many dominoes. The domino theory followed from the notion that the United States had lost China, and its logic, which transcended histories and cultures, was that of the imperial isolationists. Similarly, the promises that Johnson and his predecessors made to bring freedom and democracy to Vietnam approached the solipsism of Senator Wherry's promise to "lift up Shanghai." Johnson was not a fool. He was far from optimistic about a military victory. All the same, he could not imagine negotiating with the North Vietnamese: they were just too alien to him. He committed American troops because he didn't want to "cut and run," and he feared that the right-wingers would use "the loss of Vietnam" as they had "the loss of China."

As that suggests, proponents of imperial isolationist policies moved to the sidelines after World War II, but elements of that thinking continued to influence U.S. foreign policy long afterward. The Vietnam War taught many Americans, including many military men, about the dangers of such attitudes, among them, ethnocentrism and blind faith in the efficacy of the U.S. military. Both Ronald Reagan and George H. W. Bush complained about "the Vietnam syndrome," by which they meant an unwillingness to use force for any purpose at all, and they vowed to rid the country of it. However, Reagan sent combat troops no farther than Grenada, and the first President Bush, having expelled Saddam Hussein's divisions from Kuwait, decided against sending U.S. forces to Baghdad for a variety of reasons, among them his respect for international law, his desire to maintain the coalition that supported his Kuwait campaign, and his fear that Iraq would disintegrate as a nation. Yet, astonishingly, the ideology that had been out-of-date in the 1930s reappeared almost full-blown as the guiding philosophy of the first twenty-first-century administration. Strains of it could be heard when Rumsfeld dismissed France and Germany's opposition to the Iraq invasion as the irrelevant posturing of "Old Europe."

By August 2001, Bush's polls were falling and congressional Democrats were confidently attacking what they saw as the aberrant unilateralism of his foreign policy. But 9/11 ended all criticism of Bush and gave the key players in the administration the political opportunity to do what they had always wanted to do.

Cheney and Rumsfeld had served in the Ford administration when the helicopters lifted off the roof of the U.S. embassy in Saigon, and among all the reasons they had for invading Iraq, putting a final end to "the Vietnam syndrome" was surely one of them. The overthrow of Saddam by shock and awe was to be as much a demonstration to the American public as it was to Middle Easterners. What it has provided instead is a demonstration model of the catastrophic consequences of such primitive thinking.

Notes

1. Among my sources for the thinking of Bush administration officials about Iraq are Richard A. Clarke, *Against All Enemies: Inside America's War on Terror* (New

York: Simon and Schuster, 2004); Ivo Daalder and James M. Lindsay, *America Unbound: The Bush Revolution in Foreign Policy* (Washington, DC: Brookings Institution Press, 2003); Peter Galbraith, *The End of Iraq: How American Incompetence Created a War Without End* (New York: Simon and Schuster, 2007); Ron Suskind, *The One Percent Doctrine* (New York: Simon and Schuster, 2006); Bob Woodward, *Plan of Attack* (New York: Simon and Schuster, 2004); Bob Woodward, *State of Denial* (New York: Simon and Schuster, 2006); Nicholas Lemann, "Letter from Washington: The Next World Order," *New Yorker,* April 1, 2002; Lemann, "Letter from Washington: After Iraq: The Plan to Remake the Middle East," *New Yorker,* February 17, 2003.

2. "Excerpts From Pentagon's Plan: 'Prevent the Re-Emergence of a New Rival.'" *New York Times,* March 8, 1992.

Chapter 4

A Motive Hiding in Plain Sight

War for Oil

Michael T. Klare

In the months leading up to the invasion of Iraq, Bush administration officials were adamant in their insistence that oil played no role in the U.S. planning for a possible military assault. "The only interest the United States has in the [Persian Gulf] region is furthering the cause of peace and stability, not [Iraq's] ability to generate oil," presidential spokesperson Ari Fleischer famously declared on October 30, 2002.[1] When Fleischer first uttered these words, the "cause of peace and stability" was said to reside in the elimination of Saddam Hussein's weapons of mass destruction (WMD). But when no WMD were found in Iraq, it was said to lie in the elimination of Hussein himself and the establishment of a democratic regime. Later, when democracy failed to flourish, it was said to entail the stabilization of Iraq and the defeat of "Islamo-fascism." As all of these endeavors have come up empty-handed, suspicion as to the Bush administration's actual motive for invading Iraq has inevitably circled back to what was widely assumed to be the original impulse: oil.

Certainly anyone who was paying close attention to the administration's planning for the invasion would have seen ample evidence of Washington's interest in securing control over Iraq's prolific oil reservoirs.[2] There was, for example, the Working Group on Oil and Energy, a cadre of pro-American expatriate Iraqi oil managers assembled by the U.S. Department of State in late 2002 to establish the guidelines for the privatization of the Iraqi oil industry once Hussein was removed and a new regime put in place in Baghdad.[3] Equally revealing was the creation of a special military task force whose primary mission was to seize control of Iraqi oil fields at the very onset of the invasion. "Without going into great detail," a senior Pentagon official explained on January 24, 2003, "it's fair to say that our land component commander and his planning staff have crafted strategies that will allow us to secure and protect these fields as rapidly as possible."[4] And if that wasn't enough, the very first military action of the invasion itself was an armed raid on Iraq's offshore oil facilities. "Swooping silently out of the Persian Gulf night," an overly excited reporter for the *New York Times* wrote on March 22, 2003, "Navy Seals seized two Iraqi oil terminals in bold raids that ended early this morning, overwhelming lightly armed Iraqi guards and claiming a bloodless victory in the battle for Iraq's vast oil empire."[5]

In considering these phenomena, it is easy to reach the conclusion that the Bush administration's primary motive was to gain control over the Iraqi oil industry and to parcel it out to U.S. energy firms. Lending credibility to this view is the fact that Iraq possesses the world's second-largest reserves of conventional petroleum—an estimated 115 billion barrels, or 9.5 percent of the known global supply—and is believed to sit atop large reservoirs of as-yet-unexplored oil, possibly boosting its net holdings by as much as 100 percent.[6] There is also ample evidence that officials of top U.S. oil companies met with Ahmed Chalabi and other U.S.-backed Iraqi expatriates in the months leading up to the U.S. invasion to discuss their participation in Iraq's oil sector once Saddam Hussein was removed and the industry had been privatized in accordance with Washington's wishes.[7] But although there is no question that U.S. oil giants like Exxon Mobil and Chevron would like to operate in Iraq if given the chance, gaining access to Iraqi reserves is only a part of Washington's motive for invading Iraq; far more significant is the geopolitical objective of maintaining control over the entire Persian Gulf region—the source of three-fifths of the world's oil supply.[8]

Bordering the Persian Gulf are a handful of oil producers that together possess an estimated 736.7 billion barrels of oil, or 61.4 percent of the world's proven reserves (as of June 2007).[9] They include Saudi Arabia, the world's number one producer, along with Iran, Iraq, Kuwait, Oman, Qatar, and the United Arab Emirates (UAE). These suppliers are important not only because they house such a large percentage of the world's known reserves, but also because they possess a greater capacity than most other producers to boost production in the years ahead to meet rising world demand. Because oil fields in the global North—the United States, Canada, Europe, the former Soviet Union—were developed earlier in the Petroleum Age, they have largely reached their peak levels of production and are now in decline; the fields of the global South, however, were largely developed later and so are still capable of producing more oil before they, too, will peak and decline. And of all the fields in the world, none are more likely to produce more in the years ahead than those in Saudi Arabia and neighboring Gulf states—making them even more important to the world economy in the future than they have been in the past.

No top U.S. official has understood all this better than Vice President Dick Cheney—arguably the principal architect of the 2003 U.S. invasion of Iraq. Cheney first revealed his grasp of Persian Gulf geopolitics on September 11, 1990, when, as secretary of defense in the first Bush administration, he testified before the Senate Armed Services Committee on the justification for U.S. intervention in the first Gulf War:

> We obviously have a significant interest because of the energy that is at stake in the Gulf. Iraq controlled 10 percent of the world's reserves prior to the invasion of Kuwait. Once Saddam Hussein took Kuwait, he doubled that to approximately 20 percent of the world's known oil reserves. Of course, within a couple of hundred miles of the border of Kuwait, in the Eastern Province of Saudi Arabia, reside another 24 or 25 percent of the world's known reserves. So, we found ourselves in a situation where suddenly, as a result of his invasion of Kuwait on August 2, he was indeed in control of the Persian Gulf's key reserves without ever having actually taken any more territory than Kuwait itself. Once he acquired Kuwait and deployed an army as large as the one he possesses, he was clearly in a position to be able to dictate the future of worldwide energy policy, and that gave him a stranglehold on our economy.[10]

Under these circumstances, he explained, the president saw no option but to deploy U.S. troops in the area to deter an Iraqi invasion of Saudi Arabia and thereby prevent Hussein from gaining such a "stranglehold." Revealingly, Cheney used very similar language to justify the U.S. invasion of Iraq twelve years later. In his most important speech on the war, delivered to the Veterans of Foreign Wars on August 25, 2002, he returned to the themes he first aired in 1990: "Armed with an arsenal of [WMD] and a seat atop 10 percent of the world's oil reserves, Saddam Hussein could then be expected to seek domination of the entire Middle East, take control of a great portion of the world's energy supplies [and] directly threaten America's friends throughout the region."[11] Again, claimed Cheney, the logic was inescapable: The United States must take military action to prevent such a catastrophe.

Seen from this perspective, the 2003 U.S. invasion of Iraq was fully consistent with long-term U.S. policy. Ever since the Carter administration (1977–1981), it has been explicit U.S. policy to employ military force as needed to prevent any hostile power from achieving a position from which it could threaten the safe flow of Persian Gulf oil to the United States and its allies. As explained by Cheney, the United States will never allow another power—other than itself—to "dominate" the Gulf or to gain a "stranglehold" over its economy. This dictum—widely known as the Carter Doctrine—was first applied to the Soviet Union (following the 1979 Soviet invasion of Afghanistan) and has since been applied to any nation that appeared to pose a threat to the flow of Persian Gulf oil.

The policy of using military force to protect vital sources of petroleum has been extended to other oil-producing regions of the world and now covers much of the planet. This effort—best described as the globalization of the Carter Doctrine—reflects growing U.S. concern over the safety of oil supplies from the Gulf and a desire to "diversify" U.S. sources of crude petroleum.[12] It encompasses such policies as expanded military aid to oil-rich countries in the Caspian Sea region, sub-Saharan Africa, and elsewhere and Central Command's daily patrols through the Strait of Hormuz to prevent Iran from closing off this major oil supply line.

With the United States becoming ever more dependent on imported petroleum, we face the prospect of a long series of wars and military interventions over the control of foreign oil. These wars are certain to claim an increasing toll in human life and will impose a severe and growing strain on the U.S. Treasury. For members of the U.S. armed forces, moreover, they will demand years of dangerous and ignoble work as protectors of pipelines and refineries. From a moral perspective, then, it is time to say: "No more blood for oil!" Surely, there is no justification for sacrificing the life of a single human being—whether American, Iraqi, Colombian, or of some other nationality—so that we might fill the tanks of obscenely fuel-inefficient vehicles with another tank of imported petroleum.

The Futility of Using Military Force
to Protect the Flow of Oil

But some might still inquire: Moral scruples aside, can military force play a useful role in protecting the global flow of oil? The answer, plain and simple, is no. In attempting to demonstrate this, I advance three main lines of argument: first, that the conspicuous deployment of U.S. forces to protect overseas oil installations arouses more animosity than it quells; second, that military force is a costly and largely ineffective tool for protecting oil installations; and third, that the very reliance placed on military action to protect oil distracts us from the necessary task of undertaking the necessary transition to a postpetroleum energy system.[13]

The U.S. experience in Saudi Arabia offers perhaps the best cautionary tale about the dangers arising from the conspicuous deployment of U.S. military forces in oil-producing regions abroad. When the United States first sought to station troops in that country at the end of World War II, King Abdul Aziz opposed the plan because, as the U.S. ambassador told his superiors at the time, he thought it would provoke "violent criticism from reactionaries and fanatics."[14] Forty-five years later, when then Secretary of Defense Cheney asked his successor, King Fahd, for permission to station hundreds of thousands of U.S. troops on Saudi territory to conduct the Gulf War of 1990–1991, he was greeted with similar concerns. Eventually, Fahd agreed to the plan—but only after Cheney promised that the troops would be withdrawn just as soon as Iraqi forces were driven out of Kuwait. As things turned out, however, George H. W. Bush decided to leave troops in Saudi Arabia in order to enforce the containment of Iraq, and this continued presence of American "infidels" in the Islamic "Holy Land" later became the rallying cry for Osama bin Laden in his efforts to recruit young Saudis for his terrorist campaign against the United States.[15]

More recently, the war in Iraq appears to confirm the view that the deployment of U.S. troops to protect oil installations often arouses hostility more than it affords protection. The United States made its ultimate priorities clear when, following the initial U.S. entry into Baghdad in April 2003, U.S. troops guarded the Oil Ministry building while allowing the rest of the city to be sacked by mobs and looters. The impression this gave—that the sole U.S. interest in Iraq was to seize its oil—has been given further credence by reports that funds intended for municipal reconstruction have instead been used to protect oil pipelines, refineries, and loading facilities.[16] No matter how hard U.S. officials have sought to affirm Washington's commitment to Iraq's well-being, nothing they have done has entirely erased the perception among a large share of the Iraqi population—which increasingly seeks U.S. withdrawal—that the principal U.S. interest in Iraq is its oil.

Much doubt can also be raised about the actual effectiveness of using military force to protect the flow of energy. Despite the many billions of dollars that have been spent to increase the security of pipelines and other oil infrastructure in Iraq, insurgents continue to damage these facilities on a regular basis, severely undercutting the government's capacity to finance itself through the export of oil. Many reasons have been given for this, including the obvious difficulty of protecting exposed and inherently vulnerable installations, the need to rely on incompetent and corrupt security forces, and the insurgents' obvious daring and determination; nevertheless, the bottom line is that every effort by the Iraqi government and its U.S. backers to enhance the security of Iraq's oil infrastructure has met with failure.[17] A very similar picture can be seen in southern Nigeria, where government efforts to protect oil installations from attack by the Movement for the Emancipation of the Niger Delta and other rebel groups have proved equally ineffective.[18]

It should be noted, moreover, that such operations are inherently expensive. Although it is impossible to put an exact price tag on the cost of global enforcement of the Carter Doctrine, a reasonable estimate would run to about $100 billion per year, or approximately one-fourth of the U.S. defense budget. That excludes the direct costs of the war in Iraq but encompasses the day-to-day operations of other forces assigned to Central Command plus some share of forces in the European, Pacific, and Southern Commands that are engaged in oil-protection services of one sort or another. Also included would be the billions of dollars in military aid to such oil-producing or oil-transporting states as Angola, Azerbaijan, Colombia, Georgia, Kazakhstan, and Nigeria. If any portion of the war in Iraq is added to this tally, the net cost of protecting oil would, of course, rise much higher.

Finally, and perhaps most significantly, all these costly and dangerous efforts represent a distraction from the main task facing U.S. leaders in the energy field: to prepare for the day when petroleum must be replaced with other, more environmentally friendly sources of energy. Although it is likely that oil will remain plentiful for another five to ten years (or perhaps a bit longer), a growing chorus of experts believe that we are fast approaching the moment when global oil output will reach its peak level and begin an irreversible decline—at which point alternatives must be available to take up the slack, or the United States will face an energy shortfall and a severe economic meltdown. Equally urgent, the United States must begin to shift from its reliance on fossil fuels like oil and natural gas to other sources of energy in order to substantially reduce its emissions of carbon dioxide—the principal source of the greenhouse gases that are heating up the atmosphere and causing catastrophic climate change.

This is not the place to weigh in on the comparative advantages and disadvantages of the various alternatives to oil, except to say that all share one thing in common: developing them on a large enough scale to replace petroleum in time to avert economic and environmental disaster will require investment on a massive scale, comparable to that devoted to the Manhattan Project of World War II or the Apollo Project. It is not likely that the United States can spend $100 billion or more per year on enforcement of the Carter Doctrine and devote a similar amount—as surely will be required—in order to develop petroleum alternatives on the scale needed. Hence, rejection of the globalized Carter Doctrine is a prerequisite of sorts for making the transition from a petroleum-based to a postpetroleum energy system.

In conclusion, the use of military force to protect the flow of imported oil is neither justifiable in moral terms nor effective in ensuring the actual delivery of energy. Instead of squandering our national wealth and the blood of men and women in uniform on the futile pursuit of "energy security" through military means, we should repudiate the globalized Carter Doctrine and embrace a new definition of energy security that relies first and foremost on the development of petroleum alternatives that do not entail reliance on the use of force to ensure their availability and that do not contribute to global environmental degradation.

Notes

1. "Press Briefing by Ari Fleischer," The White House, October 30, 2002, electronic document accessed at www.whitehouse.gov on August 13, 2007.

2. For a summary of these endeavors, see Michael T. Klare, *Blood and Oil: The Dangers and Consequences of America's Growing Dependency on Imported Petroleum* (New York: Metropolitan Books, 2004), pp. 98–101.

3. See Chip Cummins, "Expatriate Iraqis Say Oil Fields Should Be Opened," *Wall Street Journal,* March 3, 2003; Warren Veith, "Privatization of Oil Suggested for Iraq," *Los Angeles Times,* February 21, 2003.

4. Background briefing by a senior defense official, the Pentagon, January 24, 2003, electronic document accessed at www.defenselink.mil on January 27, 2003.

5. James Dao, "Navy Seals Easily Seize 2 Oil Sites," *New York Times,* March 22, 2003.

6. Proven reserves are from BP, *Statistical Review of World Energy, June 2007*

(London: BP, 2007), p. 6. For discussion of Iraq's long-term potential, see U.S. Department of Energy, Energy Information Administration (DOE/EIA), "Iraq," Country Analysis Brief, June 2006, electronic document accessed at www.eia. doe.gov/emeu/cabs/Iraq/Background.html on August 13, 2007.

7. See sources in note 3 above and Dan Morgan and David B. Ottaway, "In Iraq War Scenario, Oil Is Key," *Washington Post,* September 15, 2002.

8. The author first laid out this argument in *Blood and Oil,* chap. 4.

9. BP, *Statistical Review of World Energy, June 2007,* p. 6.

10. U.S. Congress, Senate, Committee on Armed Services, *Crisis in the Persian Gulf Region: U.S. Policy Options and Implications,* Hearings, 101st Cong., 2nd Sess. (Washington, DC: U.S. Government Printing Office, 1990), pp. 10–11.

11. From the transcript of Cheney's address in the *New York Times,* August 26, 2002. On Cheney's pivotal role in launching the war, see James Harding, "The Figure in the White House Shadows Who Urged the President to War in Iraq," *Financial Times,* March 22–23, 2003.

12. The author first advanced this argument in Klare, *Blood and Oil,* pp. 132–145.

13. The author first laid out these arguments in Michael T. Klare, "The Futile Pursuit of 'Energy Security' by Military Means," *Brown Journal of World Affairs,* vol. 13, no. 2 (Spring/Summer 2007), pp. 139–153.

14. U. S. State Department, "William A. Eddy to Secretary of State Byrnes, July 8, 1945," in *Foreign Relations of the United States, 1945,* vol. 8, p. 925.

15. For background on these events, see Klare, *Blood and Oil,* pp. 50–55; Bob Woodward, *The Commanders* (New York: Simon and Schuster, 1991), pp. 253–256, 258–261.

16. See David S. Cloud and Greg Jaffe, "U.S. Diplomat Wants More Funds for Iraqi Security, *The Wall Street Journal,* August 30, 2004.

17. See Eric Watkins, "Corruption, Sabotage Hinder Iraq's Postwar Efforts," *Oil and Gas Journal* (May 2, 2005), pp. 36–37; T. Christian Miller, "Oil Sabotage Threatens Iraq Economy, Rebuilding," *Los Angeles Times,* September 18, 2004; Robert F. Worth and James Glanz, "Oil Graft Fuels the Insurgency, Iraq and the U.S. Say," *New York Times,* February 5, 2006.

18. See "Pouring Trouble on Oily Waters," *The Economist,* January 21, 2006, p. 47; "Nigerian Militants Assault Oil Industry, Abducting 9 Foreigners," *New York Times,* February 19, 2006; Lydia Polgreen, "Armed Group Shuts Down Part of Nigeria's Oil Output," *New York Times,* February 25, 2006.

Chapter 5

To Avoid Future Iraq-Style Quagmires, Reduce U.S. Global Military Presence

Ivan Eland

The dismal failure of the U.S. occupation of Iraq offers an opportunity to seek significant change in U.S. global policies.

After every military fiasco in U.S. history, a period of retrenchment has occurred. During those subsequent periods, U.S. politicians, responding to the revulsion of the American public, have stifled, at least for a while, their desire to conduct major military interventions into the affairs of other nations.

Although the entry of the United States into World War I pushed the conflict into the victory column for the allied side, the American public became appalled and disillusioned by carnage not seen since the Civil War, profiteering by U.S. arms merchants, and the greed exhibited by British and French allies in demanding exorbitant reparations from Germany and expanding their empires by incorporating the imperial possessions of the vanquished. These outcomes severely undermined Woodrow Wilson's idealistic rhetoric that the war would "make the world safe for democracy." Thus, in the subsequent administrations of Warren Harding, Calvin Coolidge, and Herbert Hoover—and even into the first two terms of the Franklin Delano Roosevelt administration—the public revulsion for unnecessary wars and foreign entanglements brought a more humble U.S. foreign policy. During this postwar period, the United States even lessened its meddling in Latin America, its primary sphere of influence.

Similarly, after the debacle of a Chinese counterattack in response to the U.S. invasion of North Korea and the resulting stalemate on the battlefield, the American public soured on the Korean War. In the two subsequent Eisenhower administrations, the president had to limit his major overt military interventions to the rather small-scale action in Lebanon in 1958.

After the U.S. military disaster in Vietnam, the Ford and Carter administrations limited U.S. military interventions to failed attempts at rescuing sailors on the USS *Mayaguez* and diplomats taken hostage in Iran, respectively. The American people's laudable reluctance to support unnecessary military intervention was pejoratively called the "Vietnam syndrome" by the foreign policy establishment, which busied itself trying to find ways to trick the public out of its enlightened "casualty aversion" to open the way for brushfire wars in remote corners of the world.

Finally, in 1993, after eighteen Army Rangers were killed and the United States was forced to withdraw from Somalia, Bill Clinton, for the rest of his two terms in office, became reluctant to intervene in foreign lands using large numbers of U.S. ground forces.

So the invasion and occupation of Iraq for flimsy reasons, the conversion of that country from a stable autocracy into a chaotic and violent state of anarchy, and the deaths of at least tens of thousands of Iraqis and more than 3,900 U.S. military personnel (at this writing) should cause the typical public backlash against foreign intervention here at home. This time, however, the respite from foreign adventures needs to be enshrined in a permanent change in U.S foreign policy. The time is right to move back toward the traditional, more restrained foreign policy of the nation's founders that the United States followed for much of its history.

The founders presciently realized that the United States was located oceans away from the world's primary centers of conflict. They concluded that the same separation by water that had allowed Britain to get by with small standing armies, thus allowing personal liberties to flourish, applied to the United States in even greater measure. The founders believed that the United States had the luxury of staying out of most permanent, entangling alliances and the needless wars they dragged allies into fighting. After World War II, at just the time that the advent of nuclear weapons made an invasion of the United States even less likely than it had been before, the United States abandoned the founders' wise policy of military restraint and began to acquire an informal empire that included U.S.-dominated permanent alliances, military bases in far-flung corners of the world, and profligate overseas military interventions.

President Harry S. Truman began the permanent U.S. empire, but chief executives of both parties continued it under the rubric of fighting Soviet communism. Belying this rhetoric as the entire reason for U.S. overseas activism, however, was the fact that the U.S. empire took advantage of the Soviet Union's collapse in order to expand. The United States stretched its security umbrella by adding ten countries in the former Eastern bloc to the North Atlantic Treaty Organization (NATO) and converting the alliance from a defensive pact to an offensive one that would provide a fig leaf for U.S. military interventions in other parts of Europe (for example, Bosnia and Kosovo) and beyond (for example, Afghanistan). In East Asia, the United States strengthened its security guarantees for its allies. Taking advantage of the attacks on September 11, 2001, and the "war on terror," the United States established "temporary" bases in the Central Asian nations of the former Soviet Union. In the Persian Gulf, it was not until 1991—after the major "threats" to Gulf oil had collapsed (the Soviet Union) or had been defeated (Saddam Hussein)—that the United States established a permanent military presence on the ground in the Gulf.

Unless the overextended U.S. "security" perimeter is shrunk, it will drag the United States into future brushfire conflicts that will needlessly expend the nation's blood and treasure and shorten its tenure as a great power. The United States is the only nation that regularly intervenes militarily outside its own region and does so in every corner of the world. Usually U.S. interventions are justified on the basis of some idealistic goal—for example, the "humanitarian" objective of stopping ethnic cleansing in Bosnia and Kosovo during the Clinton administration or spreading democracy in Iraq during the George W. Bush administration.

Yet in the last century, the only U.S. intervention with genuine humanitarian aims may have been in Somalia during 1992 and 1993 by the George H. W. Bush and Clinton administrations. Even this attempt to change the culture of violence in a society with foreign customs and norms—using violence—ended in failure. In the wake of failure in Somalia, the Clinton administration passed up taking action in the deadliest conflict of all—the

Rwandan genocide. As for the interventions in Bosnia and Kosovo, they were not undertaken primarily for "humanitarian" reasons, but rather to stabilize Europe and to give the NATO alliance something to do after the collapse of the Soviet Union.

Illustrating that bringing democracy to Iraq was not the primary goal of George W. Bush's invasion of that country was his grudging willingness to allow direct elections only after Ayatollah Ali al-Sistani, Iraq's Shiite spiritual leader, organized massive public demonstrations that demanded such a vote. Previously, the Bush administration had wanted to indirectly select friendly Iraqi leaders through a less than democratic caucus system. In reality, according to Bush's deputy secretary of defense, Paul Wolfowitz, a principal architect of the Iraq invasion, one of the main reasons for the invasion was that Iraq was awash in oil. Yet many economists would say that "defending" oil that will flow to the wealthy West anyway, because it is profitable to export, is neither necessary nor cost-effective. Thus, perhaps the real U.S. goal was to control the flow of oil to competing regions and nations—for example, Europe, China, and India.

Therefore, pledging to "defend" specific regions, nations, or resources by creating U.S.-dominated alliances, establishing military bases, and conducting numerous interventions could enmesh the United States in future quagmires similar to Iraq. U.S. military adventures overseas may now be even less likely to succeed because the Vietnam and Iraq wars have shown adversaries how to beat the powerful United States—using guerrilla warfare and terrorist attacks.

In Europe, a resurgent Russia, cornered by NATO expansion up to its borders and angered by U.S. bases in the Central Asian nations of the former Soviet Union, could eventually lash out at an alliance member, thus obligating the United States to fight a great power with nuclear weapons. The same could happen with the security guarantees that the United States has provided to Japan, South Korea, the Philippines, and, informally, to Taiwan, should any of them run afoul of the surrounded and nuclear-armed China. In the Middle East, by supporting Israel and Saudi Arabia versus Iran, the United States could end up in conflict with a future nuclear weapons state.

In all these regions, most U.S. allies are now much wealthier than their potential foes. These countries can afford to do more for their own defense, but they do not because no incentive exists when another nation is subsidizing their security. In Europe, the European Union could strengthen its military capabilities and be the first line of defense against any resurgent Russia. In Asia, India, Japan, Taiwan, South Korea, the Philippines, Thailand, Indonesia, Malaysia, Australia, and New Zealand could band together to be the first line of defense against a rising China. In the Middle East, the nuclear-armed Israel and Saudi Arabia (leading other rich Persian Gulf oil states) could both be counterweights to Iran.

Such new regional defense arrangements would allow the United States to retract its security perimeter and become a balancer of last resort—assisting only if the equilibrium of power in one or more of the regions was perverted by a rising or resurgent hegemonic power. This balancer-of-last-resort strategy would comport more with the more restrained foreign policy the founders thought appropriate for a republic. They realized that, as in ancient Rome, foreign adventures eroded the republic at home and converted it into an empire.

In the modern world, the cold war and the accompanying sporadic hot wars eroded unique American civil liberties and, by creating an imperial presidency, warped the checks and balances central to the U.S. Constitution. Since 2001, the war on terror has replaced the cold war as a permanent war that threatens republican institutions. Osama bin Laden and al-Qaeda, the people who perpetrated the 9/11 attacks, hate the U.S. military presence in the Persian Gulf and U.S. support for autocratic Arab governments there. Now that there is no rival superpower, the main threat to U.S. security comes from this group. Although terrorists are harder to deter than nation-states with home addresses, the informal U.S. empire and its concomitant foreign adventurism motivate al-Qaeda's attacks. If any doubt exists about this conclusion, bin Laden's writings and polls of the Arab and Muslim world bear out this dirty little secret. And if there is any doubt that a lower U.S. military footprint overseas and more humble foreign policy would reduce anti-U.S. terrorism at home and abroad, the example of Lebanon during the early 1980s is illustrative. While U.S. troops were stationed in Lebanon, the Shiite group Hezbollah attacked U.S. targets and kidnapped U.S. personnel there. After the Marine barracks was blown up and Ronald Reagan withdrew U.S. forces, Hezbollah attacks on U.S. forces dissipated dramatically.

U.S. interventionist foreign policy helps generate terrorism, which causes restrictions on civil liberties in the United States. Although deaths from terrorist attacks are certainly tragic, the erosion of the republic is probably an even greater ill. The war on terror has brought the unlimited detention of Americans without trial, unconstitutional wiretapping at home, torture, and major distortions of the Constitution by unparalleled claims of executive power for the commander in chief during wartime.

Now that the cold war is over and the rival superpower is in the dustbin of history, the advantages of maintaining an outdated and expensive global military presence have been reduced. Indeed, the disadvantages of an interventionist foreign policy have mushroomed greatly: blowback at home and abroad, the erosion of the republic, and the use of guerrilla and terrorist tactics against U.S. forces abroad. In sum, empire does not equal security for the United States, its territory, and its citizens—the main function that the U.S. government is supposed to be providing. In fact, empire is undermining such security.

The founders' foreign policy of military restraint was undertaken and survived for 170 years because the advantageous geography of the United States against a foreign invasion allowed that luxury. Even in the age of intercontinental terrorism, this geography provides advantages against terrorist strikes (North America has suffered the fewest attacks of any continent), but those incidents would be dramatically reduced if the United States didn't stir up the hornets' nest by unnecessarily meddling overseas to maintain its informal global empire. To improve U.S. security, and reduce the current overextension that threatens to erode U.S. status as a great power, readopting the founders' more humble foreign policy is now a necessity rather than a luxury.

Ways and Means

Chapter 6

Hidden Wounds
and Accounting Tricks

Disguising the True Costs

Joseph Stiglitz and Linda Bilmes

All public policy choices—including war making—involve a tradeoff of costs and benefits. It may be impossible to place a price on the expected benefits—such as "democracy" and "freedom." But costs can be estimated and quantified.

Those willing to undertake a war are always those who are most optimistic about the benefits and most likely to underestimate true costs. Accordingly, one should always subject the claims of war advocates to severe scrutiny, forcing them to lay out different scenarios, with probabilities associated with each. Only that will give a sense of how high the costs could be. In the case of Iraq, not only did its advocates underestimate the true costs, but they have attempted to keep down the apparent costs of the war in order to make it more politically palatable. In doing so, they may have increased the real costs.

In January 2006 we estimated the total costs of the war at $1 trillion to $2 trillion. We argued that those estimates were conservative, and subsequent events have supported those claims: costs have continued to increase far faster than we projected. We now estimate that the total cost of the conflict will exceed $3 trillion.

Here we review the lessons of the Iraq war that relate to the economic and financial costs and how we account them. Some of those lessons are standard lessons of economics that have been ignored in the important area of defense economics. Some of the lessons are old lessons of war. And some of the lessons are new lessons to be learned from the tragic experience in Iraq.

Lesson 1: The True Cost of the War in Both Blood and Treasure Must Not Be Hidden from View

By fighting the war with an all-volunteer army bolstered by thousands of contractors, the administration has been able to make the cost in blood seem like a financial cost—how much soldiers and contractors are paid. And then by borrowing the money to wage it, the United States has been able to hide this financial cost—which is deferred and passed on to the next generation.

The Iraq war has, in a sense, been financed entirely by borrowing. Taxes have not been raised to pay for it—in fact, taxes on the rich have actually fallen. Deficit spending gives the illusion that the laws of economics can be repealed and that there are no economic trade-offs—that we can have both guns and butter. Of course, the laws of economics have not been repealed. The costs of the war are just postponed, possibly to another generation.

Much of the discussion in the remainder of this chapter is directed at understanding the techniques by which this is done, the motives for doing so, and the consequences. It is hoped that these understandings will reduce the scope for the deliberate manipulation of information concerning the anticipated and ongoing costs of war.

Lesson 2: Volunteer Armies in Societies with High Levels of Inequality May Be Especially Conducive to Undertaking Risky Wars

When those fighting in the military do not come from the decision-making elites of society, the costs of any conflict may not be fully understood and fully taken into account when decisions are made. One might be able to rationalize such behavior by saying that the individuals chose to serve in the armed forces. But frequently the young men and women did not fully understand the nature of the contracts into which they were entering; many, if not most, did not understand that their deployments could be extended involuntarily.[1] That is especially true in the case of those in the National Guard, few of whom believed they would become frontline troops in a foreign war. If the private sector engaged in similar recruiting activities, they might be called to account for deceptive practices. At the very minimum, so long as we continue to maintain a voluntary army, those signing up should be made fully aware of all the risks (including the risk of not being able to leave the military at the time specified by the contract).

Lesson 3: The Costs of War Continue Long After Combat Has Ceased, but These Costs Are Hidden by the Government's "Cash" Accounting System

In most areas of public policy, actions taken today have costs and benefits that last long into the future. The decision to go to war is no different. It entails a commitment not only to pay the daily costs of battlefield operations but to provide long-term medical and disability care to wounded soldiers; to replace depleted military equipment; and to recruit, equip, and train a large number of new soldiers to replace soldiers and officers lost by the military as a result of death, injury, or decisions not to reenlist.

Because of the way the U.S. government reports expenditures, the costs of the war as reported are extremely misleading. The government uses "cash" accounting—a method that recognizes only the expenditures actually spent each year. By contrast, all publicly traded companies—no matter how small—must use "accrual" accounting. Under these rules, costs already incurred but not yet paid must be reported. For example, a business that promises to pay a fixed pension to its workers has to report that liability in its accounts. In addition, accrual accounting requires that capital equipment (computers, vehicles, buildings) be depreciated over its economic life.

In the Iraq war, there are two large accrued liabilities in the form of health care costs and future disability payments to veterans. These two items—in today's dollars—mean an additional $300 to $550 billion, depending on how long the war lasts and how many veterans claim the benefits to which they are entitled. In other words, this hidden cost could well equal the total reported cost of combat operations to date.

In addition, fierce combat operations have dramatically reduced the economic life of military equipment. In an accrual accounting system, the auditors would insist on a large increase in depreciation costs as planes, tanks, helicopters, and so forth are rapidly worn out and written off. And even that might underestimate the true cost if new military hardware is more expensive than the old. But none of these costs appear in the government's accounts until the bills are actually paid.

It is also becoming apparent that the length and ferocity of the Iraq war will require a substantial expenditure to "reset" the military in the form of recruiting, training, and restoring full military strength and morale to a force worn down by prolonged deployments. A prolonged and expensive exercise of this type was necessary after Vietnam.

All these costs are large and very real. There is no chance the government will refuse care for veterans, at least officially, or decline to replace worn-out helicopters. But in the cash-based accounting system, they simply don't show up yet. The result is that the total budgetary costs of the war are completely underestimated. The public and Congress often seem to be basing their cost-benefit calculations on the widely reported amount of $500 billion. But this figure reflects just the running costs of the war. The true budgetary costs—costs that the government has already accrued but not yet paid—are more than double and possibly triple that amount. They are presented in Table 6.1.

Lesson 4: Even the Ongoing Costs of War Have Been Chronically Underestimated

Before the Iraq war started, then Defense Secretary Donald Rumsfeld predicted that the war would cost $60 billion. In a taped interview he dismissed as "baloney" an estimate by Lawrence Lindsay, head of the National Economic Council, that it might total $200 billion.[2] Deputy Secretary Paul Wolfowitz even went so far as to suggest that the postwar reconstruction would pay for itself through increased oil revenues.

Not only were the original estimates incorrect, but throughout the conflict, the Pentagon has failed to anticipate the continual increase in the monthly cost. The cash cost directly attributable to the war alone has risen from $4.4 billion per month in 2003 to nearly $12 billion per month by 2007.

One difficulty in estimation is that many costs do not rise in a linear fashion according to the number of troops. The worsening security situation means it now costs more to renew contracts with private contractors,

Table 6.1. Budgetary Only Cost of Operations Iraqi Freedom (OIF) and Enduring Freedom (OEF) (not including economic costs or cost of interest on debt[a])

Budgetary Item	U.S. $ billion
Spent to date (combat operations)	605
Excess increase in defense budget to date[b]	108
Total spent to date	713
Estimated long-term costs:	
Future running costs (including surge)[c]	677
Veterans disability costs[d]	117
Veterans medical costs[e]	260
Veterans Social Security Disability pay[f]	35
Military equipment replenishment[g]	67
Military reset costs[h]	89
Total Budgetary Only Cost Estimate	2.0 Trillion

a. Interest on the debt is estimated to cost an additional $200 to $600 billion, depending on borrowing rates and repayment schedule. These costs are considered "transfer payments" and therefore typically are not included in economic estimates, though they represent another cash cost that the U.S. government must pay out of its annual budget.

b. Since 2002, the Defense budget that is not directly related to OIF/OEF has risen by a cumulative amount of $325 billion. Comparing this to the rate of annual increase over the preceding two decades, we would have expected this increase to be only $217 billion. We estimate that this additional increase of $108 billion is attributable to costs that are indirectly related to the war operations, including the cost of additional recruiters, recruiting advertising and development, additional procurement, training, support operations, contracting personnel, and other costs. We have not included further projections for this cost. As just one example, the war has made it much more difficult for the military to recruit, forcing it to pay large bonuses.

c. Future running costs based on continued U.S. presence in the Iraq theater through 2010 (minimum) and 2015 (maximum), using CBO projections for troop deployment levels, including the minimum surge in troops of 6 months. Note that some recent discussions have talked about the possibility of a permanent presence in Iraq, along the lines of that in Korea. The upper bound on the costs could thus be substantially higher than the costs in Table 6.1.

d. Bilmes, Linda, "Soldiers Returning from Iraq and Afghanistan: The Long-term Cost of Providing Veterans Disability and Medical Care," Kennedy School of Government Working Paper, January 2007.

e. Ibid., minimum cost adjusted for CBO estimates that average cost of treatment per veteran equals $2600/per annum, based on 2006 VA budget submission.

f. Estimate based on 12,219 soldiers listed by DOD as "wounded, not returned," who are likely eligible for Social Security Disability pay in addition to disability benefits from the Veterans Benefits Administration; using an average benefit of $900 per month, and assuming that 50% of those eligible eventually apply.

g. Cost of replacing military hardware and equipment that is being used up at an average of 6 times the peacetime rate; and depreciation of stock; including replacement of $24 billion worth of National Guard equipment.

h. This refers to the costs of returning the military forces to their pre-war strength, including demobilization costs, additional training costs, re-equipping mobile ready stocks, and cost of retraining and replenishing prewar strength of Reserves and National Guards.

who face increased security costs and must pay their workers higher wages to compensate for the increased danger. In addition, an increasing reliance on Reservists and the National Guard (who now make up some 40 percent of the forces in Iraq and Afghanistan) pushes up direct costs: for example, the government must pay reservists a full-time annual wage, combat pay, and bonuses, instead of paying for one weekend per month. (Using them as soldiers in these theaters also increases the indirect costs to the economy, because reservists are no longer available to their employers to perform their regular civilian jobs.)

This chronic underestimation has continued throughout this war. In January 2007, the administration estimated that it would cost $5.6 billion to deploy an additional 21,000 troops for the proposed "surge" in troop levels. But this estimate referred only to the cost of deploying combat troops for four months. According to an April 2007 study by the nonpartisan Congressional Budget Office (CBO), the surge would also require deployment of 15,000–28,000 combat support troops, which would raise the cost to at least $11 billion (for four months). The costs would rise to $27 to $49 billion if the surge continued for twelve to twenty-four months as it has now.[3] Even that CBO estimate did not take into account any of the long-term costs for veterans and replacement equipment described above. Nor did it include the implications of the surge (which CBO pointed out in a separate report)—the reduced availability of U.S. troop brigades for other potential conflicts for a period well beyond the actual deployment.[4]

Lesson 5: When the War Is Unpopular, There Is an Incentive to Use Budgetary Tricks to Hide the Total Cost

The administration has employed a number of tactics to avoid accountability and shield war costs from proper congressional oversight. The first has been the unprecedented use of "emergency supplemental" budget authority to provide funding for the ongoing operations of the war. This authority exists in order to provide funding for unforeseen emergencies (i.e., Hurricane Katrina) or new programs enacted during the fiscal year. Therefore, the only appropriate use of emergency funding would have been the original legislation authorizing the war in 2003.[5]

But the administration proposed, and Congress approved (almost unanimously), a series of eleven subsequent supplemental appropriations between the years of 2003 and 2006, totaling some $479 billion in funding for Operations Iraqi Freedom, Enduring Freedom, and Noble Eagle.[6]

This method of funding had several negative effects. First, it enabled the United States to hide the cost of the war, because the funds did not compete head-on with regular appropriations for other governmental functions. Had the administration been forced to include the $89 billion per year in regular appropriations, the costs would have been more transparent, and the trade-offs obvious: it would be clear that if taxes were not raised or other expenditures cut, the deficit would have soared even higher.

More importantly, using the emergency funding route allowed the administration to submit hastily assembled funding requests instead of following the annual budget process. The result was that the very people within the government whose job it is to analyze budget requests—budget analysts in the Office of Management and Budget, as well as congressional budget analysts—were prevented from doing so. Their lack of involvement in the budgetary process for the war was one of the factors that led to cost overruns in contractor operations, overpayments to Halliburton, and confusion over funding.[7]

A second important budgetary "trick" has been to shift some of the costs from "war" to general military appropriations. Between 2002 and 2007, the military budget outside of expenditures for Iraq and Afghanistan has increased by $325 billion. Of this amount, about $115 billion, or one-third of the total, cannot be attributed to ordinary increases in personnel, procurement, and inflation or otherwise attributed directly to the war on terrorism. The U.S. government is not spending substantially more money on developing new weapons systems. Overall defense spending since the beginning of the war has increased much faster than would be predicted by its average annual increase over the past thirty years. Arguably, most of this increase in spending is related in one way or another to the wars in Iraq and Afghanistan.

A third technique has been to defer spending on maintenance and replacement of equipment until after the war is over. This lowers the apparent cost of the war, and allows costs to be deferred and shifted into the general defense budget. An example is the situation facing the Air Force fleet, which is older than ever and wearing out faster because of heavy use in Iraq and Afghanistan. The Air Force now spends 87 percent more on maintenance for a fleet of warplanes than it did ten years ago, due to a larger number of missions, harsh flying conditions, and the age of the planes (twenty-four years old, compared with twenty-one years old in 2001).[8] The Air Force is seeking to purchase new aircraft to lower the average age of its fleet to fifteen years, at a cost of some $400 billion over the next two decades. But this long-term cost of the war is disguised as ordinary military replenishment.

Lesson 6: The Use of Contractors Disguises the True Number of Military Assigned to the War Theater

The use of contractors drives up short-term costs, since contractors are frequently paid more than military personnel.[9] Why do it? First and most important, using contractors makes it possible to hold down the headline number of troops deployed in the field. Second, the military is already struggling to keep up with its recruitment goals and is being obliged to spend considerably more (in the form of signing bonuses and incentives) to attract and retain soldiers. Third, contractors have no entitlement to long-term medical and disability benefits from the government. Finally, the use of private contractors may increase the constituency for war by expanding the number of people who benefit from it.

There are good reasons that countries do not privatize their military. The general theory of privatization outlines the conditions under which privatization of a traditionally provided public service is desirable.[10] It makes sense for governments to privatize steel mills; it may even make sense to privatize natural monopolies like electricity or gas, provided adequate regulatory frameworks are put into place. It does not make sense to privatize the military.

Part of the argument for privatization is that it encourages customer responsiveness. The makers of steel can enhance their profits by producing steel products that are more to the liking of their customers, of higher quality and greater reliability. But those who interact with the military contractors typically do not do so voluntarily; there is no market where they can choose to be interrogated by a contractor from the United States or by some other provider. Indeed, the incentives are perverse. The incentives of the contractor are to minimize costs, and those incentives do not take into account the broad range of public objectives of the United States.

To cite one obvious example: in the aftermath of the war, the United States had a strong incentive to restore the economy of Iraq, which entailed creating jobs as rapidly as possible. Young, unemployed, armed men can be (literally) explosive. The U.S. government should have done everything possible to ensure that Iraqis had a direct economic interest in the success of the occupation and that they were convinced it would be successful. But the contractors' interests were in minimizing costs. Thus if Nepalese workers were cheaper than Iraqi workers, Nepalese workers were hired. Not only did that engender resentment (especially when it was believed that at least some of those practices were being paid for by Iraqi oil money), but also spending money on those from outside the country did not create the multiplier effects that could have helped engender growth.

Lesson 7: The Attempt to Keep Budget Costs in Check May Simply Lead to a Substantial Increase in the Discrepancy Between Budgetary and Social Costs

Budgetary costs represent only part of the total costs of war to society.

Consider, for example, a veteran who is 100 percent disabled. He or she will receive about $44,000 in annual benefits from the Veterans Administration (VA), and additional benefits of perhaps $15,000 to $25,000 from Social Security disability pay.[11] But that does not take into account the often substantial health care costs borne by the individual and his family in caring for him; nor does it fully compensate for pain and suffering for the veteran and his family or the loss of economic value caused by the disability.

In this war, the military compensates families of the deceased by paying $500,000, including a "death gratuity" and payments from a life insurance policy. But these death benefits are but a fraction of even a narrowly defined economic value of life. In other situations, such as environmental and workplace accidents, the U.S. government estimates that value at more than $6 million. Compensation is typically far greater when the individual is injured or killed in an ordinary automobile accident or an accident in the private workplace.

Other social costs include the difference in pay between what reservists and National Guard earn in the military and in their ordinary jobs. Although some studies have shown that some individuals earn higher wages in the military, these studies often do not include the full range of economic benefits that accrue to a worker participating in gainful employment in his or her community and almost certainly do not include the loss in first-responder capability to that community caused by deploying the person to Iraq.

The distinction between budgetary and overall costs is not only conceptually important but also quantitatively significant. At the time of our 2006 study, we estimated that the difference represented an additional $187 billion to $305 billion in costs to society.

Although ordinarily departments struggle to expand their budgets, in wartime, the Department of Defense may attempt to shift costs to other departments, which obfuscates the overall costs of war. And all government agencies, facing budget restrictions, try to shift costs to later administrations and to the public. For example, if the VA has not planned for the number of returning soldiers who require health care, the cost of additional personnel is borne by the VA, but the personal cost of waiting in a line for hours, facing delays, and traveling hundreds of miles to seek medical care is borne by individuals in society.

Lesson 8: War Can Have Major Macroeconomic Consequences

World War II, which was widely given credit for having helped the world emerge from the global Depression, led to a widespread view that wars are good for the economy because of the economic stimulus they provide. But there are always ways of providing such a stimulus with better social and long-term economic benefits. Wars should never be justified solely on the basis of their positive economic effects.

No matter what efforts are made to minimize their domestic impact, wars have a large number of potential ramifications. And there are always great uncertainties, which can dampen the economy. The Iraq war posed substantial risks of an increase in the price of oil, given the importance of the Middle East in the supply of oil, the risk of a breakout of civil strife in Iraq, and the risk of a disturbance in one part of the Middle East spreading elsewhere.

Those favoring the war had argued that it was the best way to secure long-term low prices for oil, but they did not plan for a scenario in which instability in the Middle East would deter further investments in the Middle East. Meanwhile, the possibility that peace might break out in the Middle East—leading to prices substantially below current prices—helps explain the lack of substantial investment in medium-cost alternatives (like shale oil and tar sands), at least in the short run. Moreover, the supply curve of oil sometimes exhibits a perverse backward bending shape, as other suppliers (especially governments) feel less compelled to expand production to meet their budgetary needs. These two factors help account for the large increase in the price of oil. Even if we attribute only $5 to $10 of the increase in oil prices to the war, we estimate the cost to the U.S. economy resulting from this increase is $125 to $450 billion.[12] One might argue that these costs are just redistributive gains to the oil-producing countries at the expense of the oil-using countries. But that is not quite correct: it would have been far more efficient, from a global perspective, to extract oil from the part of the world that has the lowest extraction cost, the Middle East. The war has had a major impact on global economic efficiency.

Wars can, in fact, have significant negative macroeconomic effects relative to any reasonable counterfactual of how the money might otherwise have been spent. When the economy suffers from a deficiency in aggregate demand, the short-term adverse effects arise from two major sources: (1) War expenditures may have lower multipliers than other forms of expenditures; much of the money spent on waging a war ends up literally in the ground, whereas money spent on building schools, roads, and infrastructure leads to long-term growth and (2) war introduces a wide range of uncertainties, such as the future price of oil; markets dislike uncertainty—and that depresses investment. Wars may also impose a temporary but costly distortion in the allocation of resources, for example, from shifting production into the production of military hardware and finding more labor overseas.[13]

Lesson 9: Pretending There Are No Macroeconomic Consequences Can Itself Have Major Macroeconomic Consequences

President Lyndon Johnson, like President George W. Bush, wanted to have guns and butter. The result was that inflationary pressures built up; the cost of wringing this inflationary impulse out of the economy was huge. President Bush has been fortunate that at the time the United States went to war, the economy was operating below its potential. Moreover, globalization enables economies to expand consumption without inflation by buying goods abroad, and the United States has been doing that aplenty. Our fiscal deficit has contributed to its trade deficit; its trade deficit means that the United States has become more indebted. The interest on the borrowing looms as a major budgetary cost in years ahead. Increased indebtedness means that the U.S. standard of living will be lower in years ahead than it otherwise would have been, as Americans "ship" goods abroad to repay what they owe.

The question is, have we already counted these costs when we counted the expenditures directly? Is it double counting to count the interest? That is an important technical issue of some complexity. In part, it can be put simply as follows: Is the shadow (or social) price of a dollar to the government greater than 1? Since raising a dollar of tax revenue costs more than a dollar (there is a deadweight loss), the presumption is that a dollar of budgetary expenditures is worth more than a dollar of ordinary consumption. This is reflected, for instance, in the high returns to government investments in research and development. As war costs increased, the government was forced to cut back a variety of expenditures in other areas, including research. These expenditures would (most likely, and on average) have yielded high returns, and hence future gross domestic product is lowered by more than an amount that reflects the interest costs alone.

This is an example of the complexity of cost accounting in second-best economics, when there are distortions. But these second-best considerations can give rise to first-order effects. It would be wrong to ignore these costs.

And, of course, the costs will be larger if we don't recognize them, so that we can take actions to mitigate them, as the Vietnam War under President Johnson illustrates.

Lesson 10: Those Undertaking a War Face a Well-Known Risk of Extending Commitments When They Should Be Cutting Their Losses

The phenomenon is known as the risk of escalating commitment, and it has several root causes. Economists emphasize that rational decision making should treat "bygones as bygones," or as they put it, sunk costs are sunk, not to be recovered. The standard aphorism puts it: don't let good money chase after bad.

The problem is particularly severe because of asymmetries in loss functions and because those making the decisions do not fully bear the consequences of their mistakes. The probability of salvaging the war in Iraq may be small, but leaders may undertake a strategy with a low probability of military success because the potential gain from saving their reputation is large (whereas if they fail, their reputation will not be much lowered). They do not bear the brunt of the costs (either the economic costs or the costs in lives).

Lesson 11: The Mistaken Calculations in This War Are Perhaps Greater Than in Previous Ones, Due to a Misunderstanding of Modern Warfare

First, the administration assumed a "partial equilibrium model," which did not take into account the fact that the supply of those fighting the United States was endogenous.[14] With a fixed supply, killing one enemy reduces the number of enemy soldiers by one. With an elastic supply, killing one enemy could actually increase the number of enemy soldiers. There is a general consensus now that U.S. actions led to an increase in the supply of insurgents.

By using models of behavioral responses that were inappropriate for the situation, the U.S. government miscalculated the consequences of actions and costs. The Bush administration expected that a U.S. presence in Iraq would create incentives for Iraqis to support U.S. efforts, but the presence of American soldiers changed the environment in ways that drove many Iraqis to oppose the United States.

In a rational model, individuals look at their life chances joining the insurgency or supporting the government. That in turn is affected by perceptions of the likely winner and what a "victory" might look like. When the occupation failed to quickly restore the economy, confidence in the occupation's likely success was lowered. As its failure to restore law and order extended, confidence further eroded. Creating large numbers of unemployed men and not taking actions that would have forestalled access to weapons strengthened the insurgency and made it more effective. Excluding former Baathists from jobs (or even good jobs) meant that these individuals had an incentive not to support a successful new government, but rather to support the insurgency. The larger the number of individuals in the insurgency, the higher the probability of its success, and the more likely it will be successful in attracting new recruits.

In any war, there is "collateral damage"—the loss of life and property of innocent bystanders. But the volume of such accidents in Iraq (and increasingly in Afghanistan) has influenced many Iraqis to believe that the United States places a lower value on their lives than it does on American lives. It is easy for the opposition to exploit such perceptions—making it easier for the insurgents to gain members. This general argument is reinforced by the fact that the United States keeps a detailed account of the lives lost among U.S. troops, but it has not acknowledged the best scientific studies of civilian deaths among Iraqi civilians.[15]

These arguments are reinforced by the failure of judicial procedures. If good individuals are treated badly (e.g., tortured), then there is little incentive to be good. One risks being tortured whether one supports the insurgency or not. What may matter is the differential accuracy of the "judicial" system. If they punish only those who are complicitous with the occupation, and Americans punish many who are not complicitous with the insurgency, individuals have an incentive to join the insurgency. (Americans mistakenly thought that punishing those who supported the insurgency would discourage individuals from joining the insurgency, but what matters is both our punishment and their punishment and, most importantly, the accuracy with which punishments are levied.)

There may be a tipping point, such that when that threshold (measured, say, in terms of fraction of the population in the insurgency) is crossed, the equilibrium to which the society converges is not the one in which groups coexist peacefully within a single country.[16]

These conclusions are strengthened once one takes into account certain other "nonrational" behavioral responses. The fact that individuals are willing to commit suicide means that the usual kinds of deterrence (threats) may not only be less effective, but may be counterproductive.[17]

The administration seems to have misunderstood modern warfare in yet another way, by anthropomorphizing the Iraqi government, treating it as if it were a single rational individual. The United States set deadlines and timetables and threatened to withdraw unless Iraq met them. The United States believed that such threats would provide clear incentives for the Iraqi government to act in a concerted way. But the Iraqi government is not monolithic: There were almost surely members of the Iraqi government who wanted the government to fail. If they believed that the United States would carry out its threat, it provided them with increased incentives to engage in delaying tactics. To the extent that the U.S. policies coincided with the interests of one group or another (or were perceived in that way), it would almost inevitably be the case that some group believed that they could cut a better deal if the United States left.

The only reason that such hard talk did not have a more adverse effect was that such threats were not fully credible. Given the problems of escalating commitment, there were good reasons to believe that the administration would not carry out its threats. And because it has demonstrated its ability to resist even enormous electoral pressure, that conviction may be growing. As in Vietnam, the battle to get American troops out becomes one of persuading the electorate that it is too costly to stay. At least some of the groups within Iraq thus have an incentive to escalate the tensions.

Lesson 12: War Can Bring About Large Changes in the Distribution of Global Income, and These Changes Can Themselves Have Significant Consequences

War, like any other major economic policy, has distributional consequences: There are winners and losers. Within the United States, the two major winners are defense contractors and the oil industry. Globally, the increase in the incomes of oil-producing countries—disproportionately undemocratic governments with high degrees of instability—has contributed to global political and strategic instability.

Conclusion

Had the war brought stability to and enhanced economic growth in the region, its defenders would contrast the cost of the war with those economic benefits. If the war had brought about a wave of democratic regimes, its defenders could arguably set those political benefits against the economic

costs. As it is, the war has brought increased economic and political instability, which has resulted in reduced growth, sectarian violence, lawlessness, rising abductions, and a deteriorating standard of living for millions
of people.

More than 4 million Iraqis have fled their homes since the U.S.-led
invasion in 2003, with at least 2 million people estimated to have crossed
the border in Syria and elsewhere and 2 million more who are displaced
within Iraq and seeking to get out.[18] They include many educated families desperately seeking to earn a livelihood. How do you measure the
loss of well-being of so many innocent people? In short, there are many
effects of the war that we have not brought into the calculations; we believe that those other effects would increase the total cost even further.
But however one brings these various costs and purported benefits into
the calculus, it is still the case that both Congress and the public need a
more accurate estimate of the true costs of the war than is provided by
the administration or is reflected in the government's conventional accounting practices.

There will always be considerable uncertainty about the costs of a war,
but the U.S. government has systematically underestimated the cost of the
Iraq war. The errors are not just random. We have explored the systematic
procedures by which the costs of the war, both in treasure and in lives, both
to the budget and to the overall economy, can be—and have been—hidden
from the public. Those who would take us into the next war should not
be allowed to repeat them.

Notes

1. More than 20,000 U.S. troops have had their deployments extended
involuntarily by the use of "stop-loss" policies. More than one-third of the total
active fighting force has been ordered to serve second or third deployments. Ad-
ditionally, reservists are being called up involuntarily. More than 5,000 Army
reservists and 2,000 Marine reservists have been ordered back involuntarily since
the war began.

2. This interview was shown on the *Newshour with Jim Lehrer,* May 23,
2007.

3. Letter from CBO director Peter Orzsag to Congressman John Spratt,
February 1, 2007.

4. "Some Implications of Increasing U.S. Forces in Iraq," CBO, April
2007.

5. Or expenditures that went beyond levels that could reasonably have been
anticipated.

6. Operation Noble Eagle refers to construction of military bases and security enhancement for existing military and governmental installations. It accounts for less than 5 percent of the appropriations to date.

7. For example, the Congressional Research Service has repeatedly complained that it cannot track where funds are being obligated, and has specifically cited $7 billion in funds that were apparently spent for the war in 2003, even though Congress never authorized this spending (CRS, Amy Belasco, 2005, 2006).

8. General Ronald Keys, head of Air Combat Command, quoted in *Air Force Times,* at a speech at Langley Air Base, Virginia, May 8, 2007.

9. Contractors' wages are typically higher in immediate salaries, but lower in terms of long-term benefits such as disability pay, medical care, and pensions. This increases the short-term cost of the war but may decrease long-term costs compared to those for active-duty forces. However, in many occupations, the military is having to match contractor salary levels in the short term in addition to providing long-term benefits.

10. See David Sappington and J. E. Stiglitz, "Privatization, Information and Incentives," *Journal of Policy Analysis and Management,* 6, no. 4 (1987): 567–582.

11. Indeed, the Defense Department seldom takes into account the consequences of its actions for the budgets of other departments, such as the Social Security Administration or the Veterans Administration. Not providing adequate body armor may have saved the Department of Defense money, but it clearly increased VA costs for disability and health. None of this is surprising: government agencies often focus on their own costs, not the costs they impose either on the private sector or on other government agencies.

12. Oil prices were $23 per barrel for several months prior to the U.S. invasion of Iraq in March 2003, and future markets did not anticipate any significant increases. For further discussion, see Bilmes and Stiglitz, *The Economic Costs of the Iraq War: An Appraisal Three Years After the Beginning of the Conflict,* NBER Working Paper, February 2006.

13. Greenwald and Stiglitz have argued, for instance, that the global economy suffered *both* when the price of oil soared in the early 1970s and when the price of oil plummeted in the 1980s. The reason has to do with complex consequences of large shifts in the distribution of income and wealth generated by such large price changes.

14. In partial equilibrium models, the behavior of others (e.g., other firms) is taken as given, unaffected by the action of the firm in question.

15. The British medical journal *Lancet* has published two studies of "excess" deaths of Iraqis (that is, deaths at rates beyond that prevailing before the war) based on statistical techniques. The most recent provides evidence that such deaths exceed half a million. President Bush has only cited studies that offer far lower estimates, in the range of 40,000.

16. Many policies may have served to increase the number of insurgents and their effectiveness, and as that occurred, it increased perceptions of the likeli-

hood of success of the insurgency, reinforcing its success. Among the policies contributing to this outcome were the flawed "judicial" proceedings; the lack of adequate care in avoiding collateral damage; the failure to prevent caches of arms from getting into the hands of insurgents; the de-Baathification program; and the failure to manage the reconstruction in ways that repaired the infrastructure quickly, reduced unemployment, or promoted growth.

17. Rational "game theoretic" models underlay the deterrence strategies of the cold war. It is clear that, for the most part, such models are of little relevance in a world in which one party believes in the virtues of sacrificing his or her life.

18. "Iraqi Refugees in the Syrian Arab Republic: A Field-Based Snapshot," Ashraf al-Khaklidi, Sophia Hoffman, and Victor Tanner, Brookings-Bern Project Occasional Paper, Brookings Institution, June 11, 2007.

Chapter 7

Lies, Spies, and Legends

The Politicizing of Intelligence

John Prados

Spies use the term *legend* to denote the story assembled to lend an aura of authenticity to an agent, along with the paraphernalia that conveys fidelity to that identity.

In George W. Bush's push to war, the legend was that Iraq posed an imminent threat to the United States because of its weapons of mass destruction and alliance with al-Qaeda terrorists. The paraphernalia consisted of the claims made by administration officials, supposedly based on U.S. intelligence reports.

The trajectory of the legend can be described succinctly: To make the war happen, President Bush and his cohorts depicted the threat as looming and perilous. They bent every effort toward compelling the U.S. intelligence community to produce the paraphernalia of legend. After unleashing war, they sought to prove the claims of legend while attempting to discredit the unbelievers. When the weight of evidence stacked up against the legend, Bush officials tried to attribute their huge miscalculation to a simple "intelligence failure." And when the public persisted in seeing something beyond a U.S. intelligence failure, Bush and those around him extended the legend with the assertions that *every* nation with an intelligence service—and the United Nations as well—agreed on the Iraqi threat.

This chapter is about the trajectory of legend. It is important to deconstruct this story before it enters the realm of mythos, because it involves national power and responsibility in a complex world. Aggressive wars like the U.S. intervention in Iraq cannot be permitted or excused, and it is necessary to understand what happened in this case.

Most aggressive wars involve a legend, and understanding how legends are constructed and rolled out—to use a marketing term to which Bush administration officials themselves resorted—can help in maintaining the informed citizenry so vital to the functioning of democracy. The Bush Iraq legend is a classic example in the genre, even more instructive since the intended enterprise failed.

There were three key moments in the prehistory of George W. Bush's Iraq war, corresponding to the widening circle of those who had to be brought on board. The first moment came in early 2002, with the U.S. military and the Central Intelligence Agency (CIA) refining their plans for operations against Saddam Hussein's Iraq. The legend began suddenly with veiled threats in February, when Secretary of State Colin Powell told Congress the administration was considering a full range of options and President Bush saying he would keep his options close to the vest. Vice President Dick Cheney spoke of "terror states" and their "terrorist allies" in the same breath with weapons of mass destruction. A month later Cheney asserted that the United States "knew" that Iraq had biological and chemical weapons and reason to believe Saddam Hussein was pursuing the acquisition of nuclear ones. Senior government officials started making references to the threat from Baghdad.

Vice President Cheney encountered opposition from potential allies on his trip to Europe and the Middle East, along with a few assurances of support. Most forthcoming of all was the British government of Prime Minister Tony Blair. The British leader visited the United States in April 2002 for a summit meeting with President Bush that sealed the compact for war.

At this writing what is apparent about the available intelligence is that all the elements that would be used later to promote the war were already on the table. Cheney had questioned reports that the Iraqis were trying to buy uranium in Niger, which led to a CIA-sponsored visit there by Ambassador Joseph Wilson to investigate the matter. In Jordan the CIA had intercepted a shipment of aluminum tubes destined for Iraq. Iraqi exile groups had supplied U.S. intelligence with information claiming that Baghdad had built mobile plants for the manufacture of chemical and biological weapons.

The veracity and meaning of the data were not clear. The Wilson inquiry itself indicates that the Niger reports were not immediately taken as accurate. Weapons experts wrangled over whether the tubes could be used in nuclear programs, while the Iraqi exiles were distrusted by the CIA. It is clear from the record that the *intelligence* remained under dispute while the Bush administration hardened its stance to assert the debated information as *fact*. In addition, in a move that can only have signaled the intelligence community that their own views were being scrutinized, Secretary of Defense Donald Rumsfeld created a unit in the Pentagon specifically to critique the reporting on Iraq and terrorism. This entity became an important participant in the selective use of intelligence and rumor to help build the case for war.

The second key moment for legend was the push for congressional authority for war in the fall of 2002. Declassified briefings of U.S. war plans show that by August, arrangements to attack Iraq were well-advanced. President Bush and Prime Minister Blair cooperated on a scheme to convince their legislatures and the public of the necessity of war. Each nation would produce a public assessment alleging Iraq possessed weapons of mass destruction. The first play again came from Cheney, who asserted in an August 26, 2002, speech to the national convention of the Veteran's of Foreign Wars (VFW) that "there is no doubt that Saddam Hussein now has weapons of mass destruction."

From that moment until Congress passed a resolution permitting Bush to use force, administration assertions of the threat from Iraq spiked. In fact, about half of *all* the Bush administration's claims of an Iraqi threat logged before the war by the top five officials came during this time period. This surge in anti-Iraq rhetoric coincided with creation of the White House Iraq Group, a key body that helped construct the public narrative used by the administration in the run-up to the war. It also marked the beginning of a stream of slick propaganda papers dressed up as statements of fact. Moreover, the various sallies took place in a coordinated fashion, as when officials contrived to get information on the captured aluminum tubes to the *New York Times* and on the same day Cheney, Rumsfeld, and national security adviser Condoleezza Rice all drew attention to the story, with Rice advancing the rhetoric with the assertion that the price of inaction could be a "mushroom cloud." This same rhetoric was used by Bush himself in a speech to a veterans group in Cincinnati a month later.

Meanwhile, U.S. intelligence on Iraq became even less certain of the threat. A project to garner information from Iraqi scientists found nothing to substantiate the administration's allegations. The recruitment of a top Baghdad official, reportedly Foreign Minister Naji Sabri, brought a direct denial that there were any weapons of mass destruction. The Niger uranium charges could not be verified by either U.S. or French intelligence, and the documents on which they were based were marked as bogus by State Department intelligence analysts. Even before the CIA reached the same conclusion, its doubts on the data led the agency to ask the British to keep the Niger claim out of their government's Iraq white paper, and the CIA had the claim excised from the Bush's "mushroom cloud" speech in Cincinnati. Satellites took pictures of buildings but failed to discover any unambiguous weapons-related activity.

In the face of these challenges to the official version of events, the Bush administration struck back. On August 15, the same day as one of the war plan briefings, Rumsfeld's Pentagon unit attacked the CIA's terrorism intelligence, which had found no connection between the Iraqi government and al-Qaeda. That summer also, Bush officials demanded the firing of senior CIA analysts who were reluctant to give them intelligence that fit their case for war. And Cheney's office repeatedly asked for reviews of the data when CIA reports were judged insufficient to the administration's purposes.

Information that the CIA cast doubt upon, forcing officials to take out of their public presentations, reappeared in later ones. Thus the Niger uranium charge, deleted from the Cincinnati speech, would be included in Bush's 2003 State of the Union address. Intelligence doubts were actively countered by administration pressure. This is the essence of the "politicization" of intelligence.

Contemplating a major war in the Middle East, Bush never asked for a National Intelligence Estimate (NIE) on the problem. The only reasonable explanation for this inaction by officials who spoke of "mushroom clouds" is that the Bush White House feared that such a report might reveal that there was no consensus that Iraq posed an imminent national security threat. An NIE was written only after it had been requested by Congress. Bush officials worked to shape the estimate in the best way possible. CIA director George Tenet was charged with framing it in a certain way and having the most malleable analysts take charge of it. Tenet also helped draw attention *away* from the NIE through a blizzard of private briefings that focused on the most alarming bits of information, encouraging congressional leaders to believe they had heard the full story.

The CIA "white paper" on Iraq, which corresponded to the Blair government's similar product, again gave the public only the most alarming details. No doubt the administration counted on public concern to supply additional pressure on leaders not to look too closely at the classified details of the intelligence. And the entire procedure would be accompanied by a litany of administration assertions that went beyond the intelligence itself. As White House press spokesman Ari Fleischer put it on January 9, 2003, "We know for a fact that there are weapons there."

There *were* intelligence failures on Iraq. One was to aim the intelligence estimate at the supposed weapons programs without placing them in their wider social context, an Iraq groaning under the burden of economic sanctions. Another was to extrapolate from old information, much of it dating from the early 1990s, when Iraq had actually had weapons programs, while discounting previous United Nations efforts to disarm Saddam. A most dangerous error was to give free reign to assumptions—the absence of evidence of destruction of weapons was taken as proof of their existence—on everything from long-range missiles to chemical and biological stockpiles. But the worst error was the failure to insulate analysts and collectors from the pressures exerted by policy officials. When his chief analyst threatened to resign, George Tenet finally put his foot down on the terrorist intelligence, but that was not until January 2003.

The last spike in assertions of the Bush legend came during the final months before the war, when opinion polls showed weakening support for the enterprise, massive demonstrations and marches across the globe were opposing war, and United Nations inspectors were finding no evidence of the feared weapons. This wave of the legend included the soon-to-become infamous "sixteen words" in Bush's State of the Union address, which gave the Niger uranium charge unprecedented public exposure, and Secretary Colin Powell's presentation to the United Nations Security Council, which brought together much of the exaggerated data.

Intelligence errors combined to generate reports that showed a more alarming Iraqi threat than was justified. But the Bush administration went even further, presenting a one-sided picture, making outright assertions of imminent threat based on very little data, and always giving the intelligence an aura of fact. Administration behavior toward the UN weapons inspections was especially problematic. Bush officials cherry-picked the UN reports the same way they did the intelligence and pressured inspectors to present a more negative assessment of what they did not find.

No weapons of mass destruction materialized in Iraq. United Nations weapons inspectors turned up nothing before the war. Saddam Hussein displayed none, used none against the invaders, and produced none that could be found afterward. U.S. and coalition weapons inspectors replaced UN experts and still encountered very little. Those events made it necessary for the Bush administration to prop up its legend. The line taken was to appeal for patience; the weapons simply had not been found yet. The same tools of exaggeration and cherry-picking were employed.

A first round of protecting the legend was to claim the weapons of mass destruction had been found after all. When a couple of trailers were captured that seemed to have chemical warfare application, the Bush people hyped the discovery for everything it was worth. New pressure on intelligence resulted in a joint CIA-Pentagon report that distorted the function of the trailers. But the trailers simply did not have the capabilities attributed to them. The more that emerged, the less weight the claim carried, until it simply evaporated.

The Niger uranium charge and the "sixteen words" became a political issue in the summer of 2003 when Ambassador Joseph Wilson revealed that his mission to Niger had found no evidence to sustain the charge. That, coupled with the International Atomic Energy Agency's (IAEA) conclusion that the documents underlying this charge had been forged, began to unravel the whole Bush manipulation. Cheney's office attempted to discredit Wilson by leaking material from the NIE and outing Wilson's wife as a CIA officer who had a role in designating him for the mission.

Despite the prosecution of Cheney aide I. Lewis Libby on charges arising from this episode, its complete story has yet to emerge. The NIE material was "declassified" on very shaky assertions of legal right and was certainly done to protect Cheney's office from the charge it had deliberately leaked classified information for political purposes.

When the massive Iraq Survey Group that the Bush administration and CIA sent to the conquered country issued preliminary findings in October 2003, the unit reported no Iraqi weapons work beyond possible paper studies and lab experiments. The White House again attempted to claim that proved the existence of the weapons. But the study undercut the charge that Iraq had been an imminent threat, and the group's final report laid out in tremendous detail how there had been no weapons.

The next evolution of the legend would be to blame U.S. intelligence, making out the Iraq war as a simple case of President Bush misunderstanding exaggerated projections. The administration worked strenuously to avoid congressional investigations of the prewar intelligence and Bush's use of it, and ultimately succeeded.

The final effort to preserve the legend came with repeated Bush administration efforts to insist that everyone, not just the United States, believed in the imminent Iraqi threat. But both the United Nations weapons inspectors and the International Atomic Energy Agency found no evidence of an Iraqi weapons threat. In France, the intelligence service rejected the Niger uranium claim. German intelligence warned the United States against believing in the data furnished by the only agent ("Curveball") who claimed detailed knowledge of the alleged biological weapons trailers.

In short, there were significant disparities in intelligence views in several countries and at the United Nations, while to a great extent such unanimity of opinion as did exist was the product of a feedback loop in which politicized U.S. intelligence guided the views of foreign services. In using the unanimity argument to defend itself, the Bush administration perpetuated the feedback loop to preserve its legend.

The Iraq war has been a tragedy for Iraq, for the Middle East, for the United States, for Great Britain, indeed for the globe. The Bush administration planned poorly, manipulated to get its way, politicized the intelligence process, and played hard to shore up its legend. And the intelligence issues are only the tip of a bigger story that encompasses the legality of the war, the destruction of a modernizing state and its replacement by an essentially feudal society, the horrors of ethnic cleansing, the incompetence of the occupation, the creation of new adversaries, and the diversion of effort from more important tasks. It is a wholly self-inflicted disaster, one doubly embarrassing for being the enterprise of a democracy. George W. Bush, Richard Cheney, and their minions have a great deal to answer for.

Greater public understanding of how these legends are constructed—paired with much greater skepticism in the media—should make it harder for the executive branch to promote unnecessary wars in the future.

Chapter 8

Media Flagstones
on the Path to War

Norman Solomon

In a country with significant elements of democracy, the public needs preparation for war. Adequate media groundwork must be in place when the missiles fly and the bombs fall and that groundwork should blend into the prevailing scenery. As the scholar Nancy Snow has noted, "In an open society, such as the United States, the hidden and integrated nature of the propaganda best convinces people that they are not being manipulated."[1] The most effective agenda building for war is apt to seem like the logical unfolding of events at a time of crisis.

The lead-up to the invasion of Iraq involved a deluge of media coverage that spanned eight months. In the process, American news consumers may have believed they were privy to a cornucopia of facts and debates. But much of the discourse amounted to the field testing and fine-tuning of a public relations juggernaut that ended up carrying the nation into war. The oft-repeated "facts" were often not factual; the standard debates were exceedingly narrow. Oceans of ink and thousands of airtime hours concentrated on disputes over how and when to go to war.

Along the way, rather than being a means to avoid war, diplomacy became a way of laying the media flagstones for war. Washington's maneuvers at the United Nations were integral to public relations efforts for domestic and foreign consumption.[2] In practice, one of the key steps toward starting a war is to go through the motions of diplomatically exploring peaceful alternatives. Such pantomimes of diplomacy help to make war possible.

Fareed Zakaria, a former managing editor of the elite-flavored journal *Foreign Affairs,* recommended public relations prudence in the quest for a confrontation that could facilitate an invasion of Iraq. "Even if the inspections do not produce the perfect crisis," Zakaria wrote in late summer 2002, "Washington will still be better off for having tried because it would be seen to have made every effort to avoid war."[3] Policymakers are often eager to "be seen" as "having tried" to "avoid war."

To that end, they're often willing to give the United Nations a chance to be relevant. Pundits in Washington are also inclined to be happy at the prospect that the United Nations might redeem itself for past inadequacies—as far as the U.S. government is concerned. "In the world of a single, dominant superpower, the UN Security Council becomes even more important, not less," Thomas Friedman wrote on November 13, 2002. The *New York Times* columnist was greatly enamored with the evident potential of the world body: "The Bush team discovered that the best way to legitimize its overwhelming might—in a war of choice—was not by simply imposing it, but by channeling it through the UN."

For many American journalists, diplomacy is indeed war by another means. Three weeks into 2003, a front-page story in the *Washington Post* closed with a quote from Secretary of State Colin Powell: "If the United Nations is going to be relevant, it has to take a firm stand."[4] When Powell made his dramatic presentation to the UN Security Council in early February of that year, he gained further U.S. media accolades while he exaggerated and concocted.[5] With a dramatic twist, he played fast and loose with translations of phone intercepts to make them seem more incriminating. And, as researchers at the media watch group Fairness and Accuracy in Reporting (FAIR) (where I'm an associate) pointed out, "Powell relied heavily on the disclosure of Iraq's pre-war unconventional weapons programs by defector Hussein Kamel, without noting that Kamel had also said that all those weapons had been destroyed."[6]

But, as far as U.S. journalists were concerned, Powell's televised speech at the United Nations on February 5, 2003, exuded authoritative judgment. He owed much of his touted credibility to the fact that he had long functioned inside a media bubble shielding him from direct challenge. It might puzzle an American to read, in a book later compiled by Britain's *Guardian* newspaper, that Powell's much-ballyhooed speech that day went over like a lead balloon. "The presentation was long on assertion and muffled taped phone calls, but short on killer facts," the book said. "It fell flat."[7]

But not on the western side of the Atlantic, where Powell's star turn at the United Nations elicited an outpouring of media adulation. In the process of deference to Powell, many liberals were among the swooning pundits.[8]

Individual commentators were overwhelmingly in lockstep with key institutional media voices. The morning after Powell's momentous UN speech, a *Washington Post* editorial was in lockstep with the same day's articles by *Post* columnists. Under the headline "Irrefutable," the newspaper laid down its line for rationality: "After Secretary of State Colin L. Powell's presentation to the UN Security Council yesterday, it is hard to imagine how anyone could doubt that Iraq possesses weapons of mass destruction."[9] Also smitten was the editorial board of the most influential U.S. newspaper leaning against the war; hours after Powell finished his UN snow job, the *New York Times* published an editorial with a mollified tone—declaring that he "presented the United Nations and a global television audience yesterday with the most powerful case to date that Saddam Hussein stands in defiance of Security Council resolutions and has no intention of revealing or surrendering whatever unconventional weapons he may have." By sending Powell to address the Security Council, the *Times* claimed, President George W. Bush "showed a wise concern for international opinion." And the paper rejoiced that "Mr. Powell's presentation was all the more convincing because he dispensed with apocalyptic invocations of a struggle of good and evil and focused on shaping a sober, factual case against Mr. Hussein's regime."[10]

After invasion turned into occupation, the media emphasis shifted to the necessity of somehow staying the course. At a pivotal stage, during the weeks just after the midterm election in November 2006, the *New York Times* news coverage of Iraq policy options was often heavy-handed, with carefully selective sourcing for prefab conclusions. Headlined "Get Out of Iraq Now? Not So Fast, Experts Say," a November 15 front-page *Times* story prominently featured a "Military Analysis" by Michael Gordon. The piece reported that although some congressional Democrats were saying withdrawal of U.S. troops "should begin within four to six months," "this argument is being challenged by a number of military officers, experts and former generals, including some who have been among the most vehement critics of the Bush administration's Iraq policies." Reporter Gordon appeared hours later on Anderson Cooper's CNN show, fully morphing into an unabashed pundit as he declared that withdrawal is "simply not realistic." Sounding much like a Pentagon spokesman, Gordon went on to state in no uncertain terms that he opposed a pullout.

If a *New York Times* military affairs reporter had gone on television to advocate for withdrawal of U.S. troops as unequivocally as Gordon advocated against any such withdrawal during his November 15, 2006, appearance on CNN, he or she would have been quickly reprimanded—and probably would be taken off the beat—by the *Times* hierarchy. But the paper's news department has fostered reporting that internalizes and promotes the basic worldviews of the country's national security state. In effect, a reporter who is pro-war qualifies as "objective," while any stray reporter who sounds antiwar is quickly tagged as biased.

In keeping with tactical fixations of wartime media coverage, two sets of figures have been of paramount importance in mainline U.S. media and politics—the number of U.S. troops stationed in Iraq and the number of them dying there. The Iraqis killed by Americans haven't become much of an issue. And news coverage rarely discusses how the U.S. occupation served as an ascending catalyst for that carnage. It's been even more rare for the coverage to focus on the magnitude of Iraqi deaths that are direct results of U.S. firepower. Typically, journalists receive—and report—just a trickle of limited information about the bombing runs undertaken by the U.S. military in Afghanistan and Iraq. The official sources have very little to say about what happens to people at the other end of U.S. bombs. And, overall, U.S. media outlets don't convey much information about the human consequences.

A news dispatch from an air base in Iraq, by Charles J. Hanley of the Associated Press, provided a rare look at the high-tech escalation underway. "Away from the headlines and debate over the 'surge' in U.S. ground troops," he reported on July 14, 2007, "the Air Force has quietly built up its hardware inside Iraq, sharply stepped up bombing and laid a foundation for a sustained air campaign in support of American and Iraqi forces." The mainstream press's failure to report on stepped up U.S. bombing indicates that far from being confined to the period in the run up to the war, media coverage continues to tilt discussions of Iraq in favor of the George W. Bush administration's public relations perspective. Strong public pressure in favor of more balanced coverage must be an integral part of any effort to prevent another unnecessary war.

Notes

1. Nancy Snow, *Information War: American Propaganda, Free Speech, and Opinion Control Since 9/11* (New York, NY: Seven Stories Press, 2004), p. 22. Snow is a former cultural affairs specialist at the U.S. Information Agency.

2. The dual discourse about the United Nations alternately involves surface deference and underlying contempt, which more right-wing U.S. administrations are more inclined to vent publicly. President Ronald Reagan spoke frankly the day after the UN General Assembly rebuked the U.S. government for invading Grenada. The vote was 108 to 9 in favor of a resolution "deeply deploring" the military intervention. Reagan responded: "One hundred nations in the United Nations have not agreed with us on just about everything that's come before them where we're involved, and it didn't upset my breakfast at all" ("He Calls it a 'Rescue Mission': Grenada No Invasion to Reagan," *Washington Post,* November 4, 1983). Two decades later, the same President George W. Bush who had made a major production out of seeking UN Security Council support for invading Iraq was pleased to tell the American public that he would never wait for a "permission slip" from foreigners before going to war. Generally, the outlooks of top officials and most pundits in Washington are predictable: UN resolutions approved by the Security Council are very important if the White House says so. Otherwise, the resolutions have little or no significance, and they certainly can't be allowed to interfere with the flow of U.S. economic, military, and diplomatic support to any of Washington's allies. And rage is audible in Washington when the United Nations fails to assist with some major goals of U.S. foreign policy. Frustrated at what he viewed as a failure to use sufficient force after disputes between the United States and Iraq, columnist Charles Krauthammer waxed apoplectic in a November 1998 essay, deriding UN secretary-general Kofi Annan as "the head of a toothless bureaucracy that commands no army, wields no power and begs for revenue." What's worse, Annan's diplomacy stalled the U.S. war machine. "It is perfectly fine for an American president to mouth the usual pieties about international consensus and some such," Krauthammer wrote. "But when he starts believing them, he turns the Oval Office over to Kofi Annan and friends" ("Who's In Charge Here Anyway?: America risks blood and treasure in the gulf, Kofi Annan calls the shots,"*Time,* November 30, 1998).

3. Fareed Zakaria, "To Free Iraq, Use a Trigger," *Newsweek,* September 2, 2002.

4. *Washington Post,* January 21, 2003.

5. For an assessment of Powell's February 5, 2003, presentation to the UN Security Council and the media coverage it generated, see Michael Massing, *Now They Tell Us: The American Press and Iraq* (New York, NY: Random House, 2004), pp. 56–60.

6. FAIR, "Media Advisory: Bush Uranium Lie Is Tip of the Iceberg," July 18, 2003.

7. Randeep Ramesh, ed., *The War We Could Not Stop: The Real Story of the Battle for Iraq* (New York, NY: Thunder's Mouth Press, 2004), p. 34.

8. In her *Washington Post* column the morning after Powell spoke, Mary McGrory proclaimed that "he persuaded me." She wrote: "The cumulative effect was stunning." And McGrory, a seasoned and dovish political observer, concluded: "I'm not ready for war yet. But Colin Powell has convinced me that it might be the only way to stop a fiend, and that if we do go, there is reason" ("I'm Persuaded," *Washington Post,* February 6, 2003). In the same edition, *Post* columnist Richard Cohen shared his insight that Powell was utterly convincing: "The evidence he presented to the United Nations—some of it circumstantial, some of it absolutely bone-chilling in its detail—had to prove to anyone that Iraq not only hasn't accounted for its weapons of mass destruction but without a doubt still retains them. Only a fool—or possibly a Frenchman—could conclude otherwise" ("A Winning Hand for Powell,"*Washington Post,* February 6, 2003). Inches away, *Post* readers found Jim Hoagland's column with this lead: "Colin Powell did more than present the world with a convincing and detailed X-ray of Iraq's secret weapons and terrorism programs yesterday. He also exposed the enduring bad faith of several key members of the UN Security Council when it comes to Iraq and its 'web of lies,' in Powell's phrase." Hoagland's closing words sought to banish doubt: "To continue to say that the Bush administration has not made its case, you must now believe that Colin Powell lied in the most serious statement he will ever make, or was taken in by manufactured evidence. I don't believe that. Today, neither should you" ("An Old Trooper's Smoking Gun," *Washington Post,* February 6, 2003).

9. Editorial, "Irrefutable," *Washington Post,* February 6, 2003.

10. Editorial, "The Case Against Iraq," *New York Times,* February 6, 2003.

Chapter 9

America's Slide

From Leadership to Isolation

Jeffrey Laurenti

Four years after the president led the nation in celebration of a mission accomplished in Iraq, Americans have experienced buyers' remorse about their country's war there. Half of the 72 percent of Americans who supported the invasion in the first flush of victory have fallen away; those believing it was a mistake have surged from 27 percent in July 2003 to 62 percent four years later. Fifty-seven percent have come to see going to war as "the wrong thing" for the United States to have done.[1]

But what was the mistake? Where did policymakers go wrong?

There is wide agreement in Washington that the United States botched the occupation—too few U.S. boots on the ground, too many Baathists banned, an Iraqi army disbanded, Iraq's social nuances ignored. But many outside Washington see a more fundamental error: U.S. abandonment of collective security for a unilaterally driven agenda.

Americans increasingly fault their leaders' penchant for unilateral action. In 2007 those surveyed indicated by a 2-to-1 margin that they prefer that the United States "cooperate with other countries [and] compromise" rather than just "put American interests first."[2] Majorities are convinced that the United Nations—where much of the Iraq drama played out—is "important to American national security" and "needed now more than ever."[3]

It was Iraq's invasion of Kuwait that demonstrated that the United Nations Security Council could work as its founders intended. Through the council, the international community upheld the UN Charter ban against aggression, authorized a comprehensive embargo, and ultimately authorized U.S. military action to evict the invader. But once Iraq's army was shattered, President George H. W. Bush ordered U.S. troops to halt their advance rather than "occupy Baghdad and, in effect, rule Iraq," later explaining:

> The coalition would instantly have collapsed, the Arabs deserting it in anger and other allies pulling out as well.... Furthermore, we had been self-consciously trying to set a pattern for handling aggression in the post–Cold War world. Going in and occupying Iraq, thus unilaterally exceeding the United Nations' mandate, would have destroyed the precedent of international response to aggression that we hoped to establish.[4]

The result of the 1991 Gulf War was a symbiotic enhancement of the credibility and authority of both the United States and the United Nations. The 2003 war has ravaged both. The metamorphosis of the United States from a global leader marshaling a worldwide coalition to win the first Iraq war to a belligerent defying most of the international community came in three stages: a division over purposes, the decision to go to war, and the collision over Iraq's reconstruction. Each step made common purpose harder to reestablish internationally.

The Division over Purposes

At war's end in 1991, the Security Council enumerated the terms of peace for Iraq in Resolution 687: acceptance of Kuwait's border; destruction of Iraq's chemical, biological, and nuclear weapons capabilities under the stern eye of a UN Special Commission (UNSCOM); payment of compensation to Kuwait and individual victims for damages sustained during the occupation; and Iraqi renunciation of terrorism. It continued the comprehensive embargo imposed in August 1990 until "Council agreement that Iraq has completed all actions contemplated" in the disarmament provisions of the resolution.

The determination of the council to defang Saddam Hussein's regime of its weapons of mass destruction never flagged, but support for comprehensive sanctions began to erode amid reports of rising hunger, illness, and mortality among Iraq's population. In 1995 Russia, France, and China began to circulate a draft resolution to lift the sanctions—a signal that some recalibration of policy was needed to keep the international coalition together.

The international coalition came under particular strain because of the Americans' evasiveness about what was required to get U.S. support for suspending sanctions. The Clinton administration had spurned overtures from Saddam Hussein to strike a deal based on "the exchange of legitimate interests,"[5] and after the conservatives' conquest of Congress in 1994, accommodation with the tyrant in Iraq became politically unthinkable. Secretary of State Madeleine Albright signaled that "the evidence is overwhelming that Saddam Hussein's intentions will never be peaceful."[6]

The rest of the world was far less invested in regime change than Washington. Iraq drew consistent condemnation in UN bodies for brutal human rights violations, but few governments would make the leap from collective censure to mandatory overthrow. The Security Council remained united in the face of Baghdad's efforts to squirrel away some of its proscribed weapons capabilities, and it drew together again when Baghdad barred UNSCOM inspectors from suspect sites as late as 1997. But a number of Security Council members became suspicious that UNSCOM might be taking too much direction from Washington, a suspicion Baghdad eagerly fueled. After one face-off between Iraq and the inspectors, President Bill Clinton himself told a questioner, "What he [Hussein] has just done is to ensure the sanctions will be there until the end of time or as long as he lasts."[7]

The realization that the United States was determined to keep the embargo in place to achieve not simply Iraq's disarmament but the overthrow of the Baathist regime drove a deep wedge between the Anglo-Americans and their erstwhile Security Council allies. Adoption of the UN oil-for-food program in 1996 mitigated the sanctions regime's lethality for Iraqis, assuaging the most urgent international concerns. But in the clashes over inspections with Hussein in 1998, the United States could only count on the backing of a shrinking minority of the council. When Washington unilaterally decided that a fierce, focused, but brief bombing campaign was needed to punish Iraqi defiance of the UN mandates, UNSCOM was barred from Iraq and unable to monitor and control Iraqi weapons capabilities. Sanctions against Iraq continued, but the Security Council would never again adopt comprehensive sanctions that a single permanent member could perpetuate, by veto, when the majority of the membership agreed their objectives had been met. The coalition that George H. W. Bush had assembled in 1991 was in tatters.

U.S. officials worried that other capitals' short attention spans and jockeying for national advantage would allow the recidivist aggressor in Baghdad to wriggle out of his box. Influential figures from the previous administration warned, "American policy cannot continue to be crippled by a misguided insistence on unanimity in the UN Security Council."[8] Those other capitals were demanding, however, what the Clinton administration could not give them: a road map to normalization with a disarmed Baath-ruled Iraq. Indeed, in the fall of 1998 the president formalized the rupture in the council over Iraq policy goals by signing the Iraq Liberation Act, which declared it to be "the policy of the United States to support efforts to remove the regime headed by Saddam Hussein."[9]

Clinton resisted the call by proponents of the policy of regime change to "undertake military action" to achieve Hussein's overthrow. But soon enough they would be in positions to find solutions of their own, in the administration of George W. Bush.

The Decision to Go to War

Within hours of the air attacks on the World Trade Center and Pentagon, officials at the highest levels of the George W. Bush administration began positioning Iraq as a front in the "war on terror." By the spring of 2002, the president had decided to gamble his presidency, and U.S. global leadership, on removing Saddam Hussein's government from power.

President Bush acceded to congressional leaders' insistence that he at least try to win international approval in the UN Security Council for military action. Bush's address to the General Assembly that fall was urgent: "We want the resolutions of the world's most important multilateral body to be enforced.... If Iraq's regime defies us again, the world must move deliberately and decisively to hold Iraq to account.... Are Security Council resolutions to be honored and enforced, or cast aside without consequence? Will the United Nations serve the purpose of its founding, or will it be irrelevant?"[10]

Bush succeeded in winning approval for war shortly before the midterm elections of November 2002. Both houses of Congress rejected amendments to condition the congressional war authorization on adoption of a Security Council resolution authorizing military force.[11] The congressional resolution gave the president authority to launch war against Iraq to "defend the national security of the United States" and "enforce all relevant United Nations Security Council resolutions."

With the United States ready to go to war, the Security Council reaffirmed its consistent agreement on the demand that Iraq readmit UN weapons inspectors and comply with disarmament obligations imposed after the 1991 war. But Resolution 1441, passed by the Security Council in late 2002, went further, finding Iraq to be "in material breach" of its disarmament obligations; affording Iraq "a final opportunity" to meet these obligations; demanding that Iraq provide "unrestricted access" by UN weapons inspectors; and vowing, in the event of Iraqi noncompliance, to reconvene, with "serious consequences" for Baghdad.

Most states shared U.S. impatience to bring closure to the standoff with Iraq, and they recognized that Americans' willingness to use military force in the post-9/11 environment could bring Baghdad's rulers to heel. If Iraq did not comply, military enforcement was inevitable. But most states voted for the resolution in the hope that the threat of force would lead Baghdad to capitulate. It did.

After four years' absence, inspectors from the International Atomic Energy Agency and the reconstituted United Nations Monitoring, Verification, and Inspection Commission gained entry into Iraq in December 2002. With Washington warning that any impediment to inspectors would be yet another "material breach" triggering invasion, the Iraqis acquiesced to intrusive inspections.

The Bush administration had scored a huge victory. Holding Iraq's feet to the fire with the credible threat of military force was working. The Security Council was united once again, and the long truculent Iraqis were humiliatingly compliant. The inspectors would soon be able to document what lingering weapons capabilities Iraq might have concealed and certify their total elimination.

Washington would have to strike the right balance between righteous implacability and patiently humoring its partners' credulity if it wanted to achieve Iraq's complete disarmament. But it was not clear that Iraq's disarmament was in fact the Bush administration's primary goal. U.S. impatience to get on with it was palpable; deadlines were determined not by inspectors' timetables but by concern that the assembling troops fight a war with minimal inconvenience from summer heat.

The Americans insisted that Resolution 1441 had set the terms and, since it had found Iraq in "material breach" of certain aspects of the resolution's terms, member states inherently had the authority to enforce those terms. But a far larger number of governments agreed with French foreign minister Dominique de Villepin that only if inspections failed could use of force, authorized by a second resolution, be justified.[12]

Accommodating Britain's Tony Blair, Washington agreed to pursue a council authorization of force. The two allies hoped for a "moral majority" of nine member states, even if that majority were legally thwarted by a veto. But even traditionally pro-American governments balked at a blank check authorization, and Washington branded a Chilean proposal for specific triggers a "hostile act."[13] In the end the British and Americans were able to muster no more than two other votes. Blaming the French for a promised veto, they dropped the resolution and went to war—preempting the UN weapons inspectors, who seemed on track to declaring Iraq free of nuclear weapons.

Most of the world saw the attack on Iraq as a fundamental breach of the peace—"illegal" under the UN Charter, as Secretary-General Kofi Annan ultimately acknowledged. Overnight, public opinion in every region of the world turned sharply hostile to the United States.[14] But in Washington's view, U.S. use of force was not constrained by the provisions of the UN Charter, and senior officials cowed domestic opposition by deriding a UN "permission slip." Still, as the Iraq war dragged on and the international resistance to U.S. purposes there metastasized into a larger collapse of U.S. leadership, debate has resurfaced in the United States about proper authorization for the use of armed force.

A Collision over Iraq's Reconstruction

The third major juncture at which the United States fatefully spurned the UN's collective security framework came in the immediate aftermath of Iraq's defeat. Despite opposition to the invasion by a number of major states, there was still an opening for rebuilding international solidarity and trust in U.S. purposes: the United States could turn responsibility for Iraq's postconflict reconstruction over to the United Nations. Just as the rupture between West and East over Kosovo had been repaired by a postwar UN administration, a UN-led administration of post-Hussein Iraq might have reconciled the bulk of the international community to the unpleasantness of the war.

President Bush would have none of it. Nor did the Democratic minority think to suggest it.

Even as Baghdad was falling into U.S. hands, French president Jacques Chirac proposed that the United Nations "take on the political, economic, humanitarian and administrative reconstruction of Iraq."[15] Washington was outraged by what war advocates saw as a blatant French move to deprive it of the spoils—and the opportunity the triumph of U.S. arms had given the United States to reshape the Middle East. A senior official asserted, "Our men and women spilled blood for this. We didn't get rid of this regime so the French can benefit from contracts."[16]

The administration saw scant need to involve the United Nations in postwar Iraq at all; at most, President Bush would invite it to coordinate humanitarian assistance to the poor, hungry, and displaced—people irrelevant to the power dynamic of the new order. But Washington did need an end to UN sanctions on the sale of Iraqi oil. In Resolution 1483, passed on May 22, 2003, the United States and Britain conceded that they were "occupying powers" under international law—and the Security Council acknowledged the reality of the occupation regime without authorizing it.[17] The United Nations would have a "special representative," tasked with "working intensively with the Authority, the people of Iraq, and others concerned to advance efforts to restore and establish national and local institutions for representative governance."[18] The trade embargo was lifted, and Iraq's oil money, which the United Nations had administered for the welfare of the population under oil-for-food, would be transferred to the control of the occupying powers—a boon because they could spend it unencumbered by the restraints applicable to congressional appropriations for Iraq's reconstruction.[19]

President Bush proceeded to establish a government in Iraq under Paul Bremer; the British had little say and the State Department had even less. The UN special representative, Sérgio Vieira de Mello, sought to fulfill his mandate through dialogue with Iraqi political factions that refused to deal with the occupying power, but within three months he and twenty-one UN colleagues were killed in a deadly terrorist attack, and the UN mission left Baghdad. Months later when the Coalition Provisional Authority found itself at a political impasse, shunned by leading Iraqi figures, Washington asked the United Nations to dispatch a seasoned interlocutor to open consultations with all Iraqi factions on the formation of an interim government. Lakhdar Brahimi's delicately balanced slate to lead the post-Bremer regime was not sufficiently inclusive of U.S. allies, however, and Bremer and his Iraqi appointees overruled the UN nominees for interim president and prime minister.

America's Slide

The American public has now become decisively disillusioned with the war. But the Washington debate indicts only the blunders of Bremer's rule in Baghdad—not the evolving decision to hold out for Hussein's overthrow, not the decision to invade Iraq in defiance of most of the international community, and not the determination to impose American tutelage rather than UN administration on the prostrate country. Each of those policy choices distanced the United States ever further from the solid international front that President George H. W. Bush had so skillfully built to overturn Iraq's aggression against Kuwait. Each of them represented a considered but costly decision to prefer a maximalist U.S. objective over the shared global objective that may have been within reach as early as the mid-1990s and that was certainly in hand in March 2003—an Iraq free of nuclear weapons.

For Americans, achievement of the goals globally agreed would likely have been unsatisfying: Even if Iraq were neutered militarily, its Arab majority would still have been left under a brutal tyrant who had launched two wars of aggression (albeit a secular ruler who remorselessly crushed any jihadist terrorism and opposed Islamic Iran). In pursuit of larger ambitions for Iraq, however, Americans have borne a heavy cost. And the cost that Iraqis have borne in their shattered country, or in flight from it, should not be incidental.

Iraq has become the graveyard for ambitious designs of twenty-first-century U.S. global supremacy. In coming years, U.S. political leaders will almost certainly have to adapt their styles and aspirations to global leadership to the international rules of the game that the United Nations embodies. Understanding the missteps on the road to Baghdad will be crucial in shaping realistic new thinking among the next generation of U.S. policymakers about future options for the United States within and without the United Nations.

Notes

1. USA Today/Gallup Poll, July 7–9, 2003, July 6–8, 2007; Quinnipiac University Polling Institute, June 11, 2007.

2. American Security Project (ASP)/Marttila Communications, *America and the World: Evolving Attitudes on Foreign Policy and National Security,* May 8, 2007: 63 percent select "cooperate/compromise" and 32 percent "acting alone."

3. According to ASP/Marttila, 54 percent find it "important," whereas 37

percent dismiss it as "flawed, ineffective, and corrupt." According to a Zogby Interactive/UPI poll taken July 13–16, 2007, 52.8 percent say the UN is needed now more than ever, whereas 41.1 percent say it has "lost its relevancy and influence" (two options that are not mutually exclusive).

4. George Bush and Brent Scowcroft, *A World Transformed* (New York: Vintage, 1998), p. 489. What Bush told the American people at the time was, "This is not a time of euphoria, certainly not a time to gloat.... This is a victory for the United Nations, for all mankind, and for what is right." Address to the nation, February 28, 1991 (quoted in *A World Transformed,* p. 486).

5. Special to the *New York Times,* "Iraq Leader Appeals to Clinton for New Relations," *New York Times,* February 15, 1993. Hussein was convinced, almost until the day the Americans delivered him for execution, that they would eventually realize that they and he shared the same "legitimate interests" in checkmating Iran's Islamic regime.

6. Remarks of the Secretary of State at Georgetown University, March 26, 1997, http://secretary.state.gov/www/statements/970326.html.

7. Remarks by the president in a bilateral meeting with President Ernesto Zedillo of Mexico, November 14, 1997, http://www.clintonfoundation.org/legacy/111497-remarks-by-president-in-photo-op-with-zedillo.htm.

8. Project for the New American Century, "Letter to President Clinton on Iraq," January 26, 1998, http://www.newamericancentury.org/iraqclintonletter.htm. Signatories included Donald Rumsfeld, Paul Wolfowitz, Richard Perle, Richard Armitage, John Bolton, Zalmay Khalilzad, and Robert Zoellick.

9. Public Law 105-338, Iraq Liberation Act of 1998, sec. 3.

10. "Address by Mr. George W. Bush, President of the United States of America," UN General Assembly, 57th session, 2nd plenary meeting, UN General Assembly Document A/57/PV.2, September 12, 2002, 8.

11. Senator Carl Levin's amendment failed, 24 to 75, on October 10, 2002. The next day the House rejected a similar amendment by John Spratt, 155 to 270.

12. "The Situation Between Iraq and Kuwait," UN Security Council, UN Security Council Document S/PV 4707, February 14, 2003; also, http://www.ambafrance-us.org/news/statmnts/2003/villepin021403.asp.

13. Heraldo Muñoz, *Una Guerra Solitaria: La historia secreta de EE.UU. en Irak, la polémica en la ONU y el papel de Chile* (Santiago: Random House Mondadori, 2005), p. 72.

14. Annan was pressed on the issue by the BBC; see News.bbc.co.uk/2/hi/middle_east/3661134.stm. Pew Global Attitudes Project, "America's Image Further Erodes: Europeans Want Weaker Ties," March 18, 2003, p. 1, and subsequent Pew surveys.

15. Inter-Press Service, "Diplomatic Rifts Form over UN's Postwar Role," April 9, 2003.

16. *U.S. News and World Report,* "End Game: Winning the Peace," April 21, 2003 (posted April 13).

17. "This affirmation was important because, by acknowledging individual liability and state responsibility for their administration of occupied Iraq, the United States and United Kingdom recognized that this remained a US-UK venture, not a UN-sanctioned one." David Malone, *The International Struggle over Iraq: Politics in the UN Security Council, 1980–2005* (Oxford: Oxford University Press, 2006), p. 205. With the United States adamant about controlling Iraq itself, governments opposing the invasion were determined not to provide ex post facto legitimation for the invasion, as Resolution 1244 arguably did for the Kosovo war.

18. Security Council Resolution 1483, 8(c).

19. Within a month of the UN's transfer of unspent Iraqi oil funds to the authority, the United States announced that only companies from countries that were part of the occupation coalition would be permitted to bid on contracts for Iraq's reconstruction. The exclusion of others was "justified as 'necessary for the protection of the essential security interests of the United States,' but it seemed designed to punish erstwhile antagonists in the Council." Malone, *The International Struggle,* p. 206.

Chapter 10

Inspections or Invasion

Lessons from Iraq

Hans Blix

The political justification given for the Iraq war was above all the contention that Iraq retained weapons of mass destruction (WMD) in violation of resolutions of the UN Security Council. It is unlikely that any other argument would have persuaded the U.S. Congress or the UK parliament to authorize armed action.

As we know, the evidence was faulty, and reports of the United Nations Monitoring, Verification, and Inspection Commission (UNMOVIC) and the International Atomic Energy Agency (IAEA) were ignored by the states launching the war. UNMOVIC had carried out some 700 inspections of some 500 different sites, dozens of them proposed by intelligence organizations, and had reported no finds of WMDs. In addition, UNMOVIC and the IAEA had expressed doubts about some of the evidence that had been presented by advocates of armed action. The pleas by the majority of the members of the Security Council that inspections should be continued were ignored by the states launching the war.

In particular, the Bush administration used emotion-laden phrases such as, "We can't afford to wait for the smoking gun that could end up being a mushroom cloud" as a substitute for hard, verifiable information. Speculation was presented as fact, as when Vice President Dick Cheney asserted that Saddam Hussein had "reconstituted nuclear weapons." His declaration was as firm as it was unfounded.

The failure to allow inspections to take their course or to seriously consider all relevant views on the state of Iraq's weapons of mass destruction programs led to inaccurate or misleading assertions, such as the claim that Iraq had acquired aluminum tubes for use in uranium enrichment, when the tubes in question were not suited for that purpose; that Baghdad had developed unmanned aerial vehicles that could be used to deliver weapons of mass destruction, when they had no such capabilities; and that Saddam Hussein's regime allegedly possessed mobile laboratories that could produce biological weapons.

The most significant distortion of the data on Iraq was the suggestion that the failure of Iraq to verify its destruction of stockpiles and chemical and biological weapons that had existed years before was proof that these weapons were still in Iraq's arsenal. In fact, such information simply indicated that the status of these weapons could not be determined without further investigation.

In March 2003 the Bush administration rushed to war, justifying its action in significant part by its doctrine holding that the United States would henceforth strike *before* gathering threats to its security were fully formed. This approach was implemented despite the fact that UN inspections aimed at determining the state of Iraq's arsenal were making significant progress and could have provided the best possible information on the state of the Iraqi threat. Indeed, the Bush administration's own postinvasion inspections, conducted under the auspices of the U.S.-funded Iraq Survey Group, concluded that Iraq did not possess nuclear, chemical, or biological weapons, nor did it have active programs aimed at developing them.

These discoveries were a case of too little, too late. The war—which has now cost tens of thousands of lives and hundreds of billions of dollars—was already well under way. If UN inspectors had been allowed to finish their work, might war have been avoided? Since these efforts were cut short, we can never know for sure, but there is a high probability that military intervention might have been ruled out under such circumstances.

In short, the primary lesson from the Iraq war is that a rigorous regime of inspections and monitoring can be far more effective in disarming a recalcitrant state than "counterproliferation" pursued via military means. Military force is a blunt instrument that may cause more problems than it solves, particularly in the absence of good intelligence about the existence and location of nuclear, chemical, and biological weapons and related facilities and data. In the case of Iraq, the combination of the *threat* of military force and intensive inspections was well on the way to documenting the status of Iraq's programs for nuclear, chemical, and biological weapons when the war cut this process short.

Going forward, it is essential that a more robust regime of inspections and monitoring be developed to address any and all cases of potential proliferation. Additional resources will be needed to implement such a system. In this regard it is interesting to note that the entire annual budget of the IAEA ($389 million) is equal to less than the cost of two days of the war in Iraq.

An important way to avoid future wars of counterproliferation like the Iraq conflict is to institute more robust systems of inspection, monitoring, and verification regarding the potential development of nuclear, chemical, and biological weapons. Granted, the Iraq case was unique in that the inspections regime was imposed after Baghdad lost the 1991 Gulf War, which allowed for much more intrusive inspections than would normally be the case. But adoption by as many nations as possible of the additional protocol of more rigorous and extensive inspections now allowed for under the Nuclear Non-Proliferation Treaty (NPT) would dramatically improve the ability to determine what activities are being undertaken by any nation of concern.

In addition, the five recognized nuclear powers—the United States, Russia, the United Kingdom, France, and China—must take urgent steps toward universal and verifiable nuclear disarmament. The bargain struck in the NPT was that existing nuclear-armed states would move toward elimination of their arsenals in exchange for a pledge by nonnuclear states to forgo developing these weapons of mass terror. Therefore, action by the major nuclear states would remove one major rationale cited by nations that have developed their own nuclear weapons outside the NPT regime.

Among the major steps that need to be taken are the following, all of which have been endorsed by the Weapons of Mass Destruction Commission, a group of international experts of which I served as the chair:

• Move toward a World Summit on disarmament, nonproliferation, and terrorist use of weapons of mass destruction. The goal of the summit would be to set a framework for reviving meaningful negotiations toward the goal of eliminating and outlawing weapons of mass destruction once and for all.

- Secure all nuclear, chemical, and biological weapons and weapons-producing equipment and materials from theft or other acquisition by terrorists.
- Make deep reductions in nuclear weapons and take all such weapons off hair-trigger alert status.
- Prohibit the production of bomb-making materials.
- Have all nuclear weapons states make a pledge of no-first-use of nuclear weapons.
- Prevent nuclear weapons tests by bringing the Comprehensive Test Ban Treaty into force.
- Continue negotiations with Iran and North Korea to achieve their effective and verified rejection of the nuclear weapon option, while assuring their security and acknowledging the right of all NPT parties to peaceful uses of nuclear energy.
- Accept the principle that nuclear weapons should be outlawed, as are chemical and biological weapons.
- Increase compliance with the Chemical Weapons Treaty and speed up destruction of chemical weapons stocks.
- Increase compliance with and strengthen verification of the Biological Weapons Convention.
- Prevent an arms race in space by prohibiting any stationing or use of weapons in outer space.

The act of pursuing these admittedly ambitious measures may be enough to reduce the security concerns of potential nuclear weapons states to the point at which they are more likely to forgo such development. In addition, the abandonment of the "Bush Doctrine" of striking first against potential adversaries well in advance of any immediate security threat could provide a level of comfort that could aid negotiations in difficult cases like Iran and North Korea.

The costly military effort to eradicate weapons of mass destruction—that did not exist—in Iraq, based on faulty national intelligence and leading to estrangement between the United States and most of the international community, can hardly encourage unilateral military counterproliferation action in the future. It would be rash to think, however, that the doctrine might not be applied in some case deemed more propitious.

Many statements by President George W. Bush and other U.S. officials to the effect that in the cases of Iran and North Korea, "all options are on the table," confirm that the current U.S. administration feels free to use force, if it so chooses, without any authorization by the Security Council, even if there is no armed attack or imminent attack.

Secretary of State Condoleezza Rice has asserted that the United States would be justified in taking action in self-defense against Iran. From this, one is driven to the conclusion that the right to take unilateral preemptive or preventive action is deemed to arise long before an armed attack or a mushroom cloud. Indeed, it would seem to arise even when the first milligrams of low-enriched uranium come out of a cascade of centrifuges.

It is hard to read this as anything but a good-bye to the restrictions on the use of force set down at the United Nations's founding conference in San Francisco—at least as regards actions to stop the development of weapons of mass destruction. This surmise is reinforced by a 2003 statement by then U.S. ambassador to the United Nations John Bolton: "Our actions, taken consistently with Constitutional principles, require no separate, external validation to make them legitimate."

How worrisome is it when Article 51 of the UN Charter—providing the right of military action in cases of genuine self-defense—is seen as irrelevant by the militarily most powerful state in the world?

A problem inherent in all self-defense taken before an attack is even imminent (and visible) is that it is based on intelligence. After the Iraq affair, we know that intelligence can be a very shaky basis on which to start a war. Iraq in 2003 was not about to launch an attack on the United States, or any other country.

The case of Iran also raises questions about the doctrine of preventive self-defense. Although some Security Council members are convinced that Iran's *ambition* to enrich uranium is part of an effort to develop a nuclear weapon, it would be hard to claim that such ambition, if it is there, constitutes a threat to peace and security today.

My conclusions are that first, in the case of Iraq, it was worrisome that the right of self-defense was claimed to justify an armed action to eliminate WMD that did not exist. Second, in the Iranian case, it would be a great setback for the world if it were to dump the UN Charter restrictions on the unilateral use of armed force and recognize the right of self-defense against some milligrams of low-enriched uranium and possible intentions to proliferate in a number of years. Third, we might welcome a Security Council that is more representative in today's world and acts in concert with the international community to reduce potential future threats to peace.

However, in my view, council decisions on concrete enforcement actions should be limited to situations that are urgent—where there is acute, not just a potential future threat to the peace.

For situations in which there is not an acute threat, the authors of the UN Charter wisely wrote Chapter VI about the peaceful settlement of disputes. This chapter is meant to cover any dispute, "the continuation of which is likely to endanger the maintenance of international peace and security."

This approach should be applied to Iran and other potential proliferators that are far from achieving a weapons capability. The negative consequences of proceeding to the use of force in the absence of an imminent threat are all too painfully obvious in the case of Iraq.

As Chapter VI of the charter suggests, there are many situations in which diplomacy will be more effective than force. Contrary to the views of some critics, the authors of the UN Charter who emerged from World War II were not pacifists. But they were also not trigger-happy. Following their lead would greatly reduce the prospects of another Iraq-style conflict.

Chapter 11

Coalitions of the Coerced

Phyllis Bennis

When the Bush administration failed in its effort to bribe and threaten the UN Security Council into endorsing its looming war in Iraq, it turned to a diplomatic move designed to trick the American people and provide political cover for nervous governments: a "coalition of the willing" to give a multilateral gloss to a thoroughly U.S.-driven war.

The "coalition" was an ad hoc grouping of governments, some of them so embarrassed to be joining the U.S.-UK effort that they refused to be publicly identified. The notion that it was a "willing" coalition of governments that truly believed in Washington's anti-Iraq crusade was never more than an illusion. Almost without exception, the so-called coalition was constructed of governments either already dependent on, or eager to win approval from, the United States. Just before the March 2003 invasion, the Bush administration claimed it had more than forty governments willing to participate in a war against Iraq without the requisite UN approval.

94

But the administration refused to provide a comprehensive list of its ostensible coalition partners: some members were publicly known, but others remained unconfirmed. Their reticence was not surprising; polls at that time indicated an average of 75 percent opposition to the war around the world. Most coalition governments made their decision to back Washington's war against a backdrop of massive, sometimes potentially destabilizing, domestic opposition.

So who made up this uneasy "coalition"? The majority came from three broad categories. First was what then Defense Secretary Donald Rumsfeld famously dubbed "new Europe." These Central and Eastern European countries hoped to gain both military benefits and economic ones, such as strengthened U.S. commitments for aid and trade. The so-called Vilnius Group issued their statement in February 2003, just weeks before the invasion, expressing their willingness "to contribute to an international coalition." Its signatories included Albania, Bulgaria, Croatia, Estonia, Latvia, Lithuania, Macedonia, Romania, Slovakia, and Slovenia.[1] All except Croatia were in line for membership in the North Atlantic Treaty Organization (NATO) but needed approval from all current NATO members, meaning Bush could block or delay approval.

The second major group was a host of unpopular U.S.-dependent absolute monarchies in the Middle East—including Bahrain, Jordan, Kuwait, Oman, Qatar, Saudi Arabia, and the United Arab Emirates. Mostly small, almost all oil-glutted, these repressive governments were (and remain) dependent on the United States for military support through arms, training, and the expansion of U.S. military bases. Close to Iraq, these governments held power precariously over populations strongly opposed to U.S. war plans, and all of them had supported the Arab League's unanimous February 2003 decision to oppose military assistance to any war on Iraq. But their reliance on the United States was strong enough that they cast that vote even while already providing bases, overflight rights, and direct staging areas for the Pentagon's Gulf buildup. In one example, Jordan was reported to be hosting U.S. Special Forces and collaborating with U.S. intelligence agents in exchange for an additional $1 billion in U.S. aid.[2]

The third group was made up of governments eager for increased aid, trade, and "security" support from the United States. Costa Rica's foreign minister reversed the antiwar position of its UN ambassador, presumably jittery over the negotiations Costa Rica was then leading on the Central American Free Trade Agreement. The Philippines, already heavily dependent on U.S. economic as well as military assistance, joined the coalition in 2003 after receiving $71 million from the U.S. Agency for International Development the year before, as well as support—including

1,700 new U.S. troops—to help fight a small criminal gang operating in the southern Philippines, which the United States suddenly claimed was tied to al-Qaeda.

The United States continued its efforts to win UN support for war from the fall of 2002 through the winter of 2003, but it was never able to do so. Then Secretary of State Colin Powell made what too many thought to be the definitive case for war against Iraq in the UN Security Council. But it didn't work—the wavering governments and, more importantly, the unwavering public opposition did not give in. The United States tried desperately to subvert the role of the UN arms inspectors, who had returned to Iraq in the fall of 2002, but was unable to gain multilateral support to do so. Throughout those months, the effort to pressure countries to join the "coalition" continued.

The pressure was most fierce on the resisting countries within the UN Security Council. Of the fifteen, only Britain, Bulgaria, and Spain backed Bush's war plans. In London, Tony Blair remained Bush's most consistent ally, ultimately paying a huge price in his own political legacy. Spain's unpopular prime minister lost the first vote in 2004 after his deployment of Spanish troops to Iraq and the deadly terrorist bombing in Madrid that followed; his successor's first act was to withdraw the troops. Bulgaria, eager to gain U.S. support for its NATO bid, granted the Pentagon use of military bases, Bulgarian airspace, and 150 troops trained in biological and chemical warfare.[3]

The United States realized it had little leverage over the strong opponents—France and Germany in the lead with Syria, as well as Russia and China standing back. But the "uncommitted six" came under extraordinary pressure. Guinea and Cameroon were threatened with a cutoff of aid under the Africa Growth and Opportunity Act if they refused to support the U.S.-UK war; an obscure line in the act barred aid to countries "undermining" U.S. foreign policy interests. It didn't define or specify those interests, but one could be fairly certain that refusing to support the U.S. war would qualify. Chile, whose postdictatorship government had just finished a seven-year-long negotiating process aimed at finalizing a U.S.-Chile free trade agreement, was informed that the White House would prevent the treaty's ratification if Santiago did not support Washington's war. And Mexico, whose President Vicente Fox had been elected on a platform rooted in U.S.-Mexico border and immigration negotiations, was told that all future negotiations were off unless Mexico endorsed the war.

The pressures were fierce. And yet all six (the others were Angola and Pakistan) refused to give in.

Only when the effort to win UN support finally failed did the role of the coalition take center stage. That failure, appropriately, became public midway through the February 15, 2003, rally protesting the war directly in front of UN headquarters in New York on a bitterly cold afternoon. An Associated Press wire story broke and was relayed backstage and read to the half-million-strong crowd. "Rattled by an outpouring of international anti-war sentiment, the United States and Britain began reworking a draft resolution Saturday to authorize force against Saddam Hussein. Diplomats, speaking on conditions of anonymity, said the final product may be a softer text that does not explicitly call for war."

It was an extraordinary moment. But it was also the moment when, without UN approval, the "coalition" was all that remained of the Bush administration to claim legitimacy—however false—for an illegal war.

It was clear from the beginning that the coalition was never designed for military support, but rather to provide political cover to the decision to invade Iraq. Only the British contingent played a significant military role, although other national forces (including nineteen Italian soldiers killed on one day) paid a heavy price in lives lost.

Very soon after the war in Iraq began, the coalition began to fray. By June 2004, soon after the so-called end of occupation by the U.S.-UK troops, the scramble for governments to get their troops out of the un-popular war was well under way. The *Washington Post* described how "the symbolic importance of international participation has been at least as vital for the Bush administration as the often-limited military role the troops have played. And while administration officials have stressed the number of countries that have sent troops, others have noted the small size of many military contingents and the continued absence of some major powers. Several participating countries sent fewer than 100 troops. In other cases, forces diminished significantly over time. Moldova's contingent is the smallest—down to 12 from 42. Singapore has quietly reduced its presence from 191 to 33.... Support is also tenuous in nations Washington considers to be key players."[4]

By August 2007, only eight countries had more than fifty troops deployed in Iraq, and the total "coalition" numbered only about 11,500 (half of those from the UK), compared to the 160,000 U.S. troops occupying the country.[5] By far the largest non-U.S. troop contingent was not the "coalition" at all, but rather the tens of thousands of armed contractors—mercenaries—backing up the U.S. troops.[6]

Certainly, the United States had used bribes, threats, and punishments before to gain international support. In the 1990–1991 Gulf crisis, China was bribed (with new development aid and normalization of post–Tienanmen

Square diplomacy) not to veto the U.S. resolution authorizing war against Iraq. Poor countries dependent on the United States and serving on the Security Council, including Colombia, Zaire, and Ethiopia, were all given new U.S. aid packages, new access to World Bank credits, and/or refinancing of International Monetary Fund loans. Colombia was given new U.S. military aid, as was Ethiopia following years of an arms embargo because of civil war. Punishments were used, too. Only two countries voted against the U.S. war authorization in 1990: Yemen and Cuba. Yemen was the only Arab country on the council. No sooner had the Yemeni ambassador put down his hand than a U.S. diplomat was at his side, saying, "That will be the most expensive 'no' vote you ever cast." Three days later the United States cut its entire (already tiny) aid budget to Yemen. The remark was picked up on an open UN microphone and ultimately broadcast around the world; to this day the "Yemen precedent" casts a pall of fear over UN discussions.

A still unanswered question remains: Why, faced with Yemen-style resistance on a much broader, even global scale, did the United States this time around fail to make good on any of its grandiose threats? No aid was cut to Guinea or Cameroon; Chile's free trade pact was duly ratified; Mexico continued negotiating over the border. The only U.S. punishment was the successful pressure Washington exerted on Mexico and Chile to replace their outspoken UN ambassadors. Two individuals paid a price. But the global resistance stood.

The Lessons

The United States launched the invasion and occupation of Iraq in March 2003 in defiance of overwhelming international global and popular opposition. The United Nations had refused to endorse the invasion, and the Security Council's "uncommitted six" countries resisted pressure to board Washington's war train. On February 15, 2003, in what the *Guinness Book of World Records* called the "biggest protest on a single day in history," 12 to 14 million people had poured into the streets of capitals around the world, united under a single slogan: The World Says No to War.

It was a stunning example of global unity against war that brought together people, some governments, and ultimately the United Nations itself. The Bush administration had fought hard and dirty to be able to claim some kind of legitimacy for its war, and when the global resistance movement made a UN imprimatur impossible, it grabbed what authority it could from creation of what was falsely called a "coalition of the willing."

Looking back, what is clear is that an ad hoc, cobbled together "coalition" cannot replace the legitimacy of the United Nations that the UN Charter requires to approve the use of force (absent a real attack legitimating self-defense). The lesson of the run-up to the Iraq invasion is that when global mobilization of people and governments successfully bolsters UN refusal to endorse a preventive war, creation of such a "coalition" does not legitimize that war. Bush's invasion of Iraq was, as UN Secretary General Kofi Annan succinctly described it, "illegal."

Notes

1. U.S. Embassy in Bulgaria website, "Statement of the Vilnius Group Countries in Response to the Presentation by the United States Secretary of State to the United Nations Security Council," February 5, 2003.

2. William D. Hartung and Michelle Ciarrocca, "Buying a Coalition," *Nation,* March 17, 2003.

3. *Deseret News,* February 13, 2003.

4. Robin Wright and Bradley Graham, "U.S. Works to Sustain Iraq Coalition," *Washington Post,* July 15, 2004.

5. Brookings Institution, *Iraq Index: Tracking Variables of Reconstruction and Security in Post-Saddam Iraq,* www.brookings.edu/iraqindex.

6. Josh Meyer and Julian E. Barnes, "Congress Moves to Rein in Private Contractors," *Los Angeles Times,* October 4, 2007.

Collateral Damage

Chapter 12

Monarchic Pretensions

The War Power Grab

Fred Barbash

The framers of the Constitution worried often during their Philadelphia deliberations about the prospect of a chief executive who engages the country in war and then exploits the inevitable fear and fervor to usurp legislative and judicial authority, effectively becoming an elective monarch. They understood, as James Madison told his fellow delegates, that "the means of defense against foreign danger have always been the instruments of tyranny at home"; that war "tends to render the head too large for the body that a standing military force and an overgrown executive, will not long be safe companions to liberty." Two and a half centuries later, the administration of George W. Bush, more than any preceding presidency, has justified their concern. Acting under his designation as commander in

102

chief, Bush sought to become the all-in-one president, assuming judicial, legislative as well as executive authority by claiming sole power to wage war, to amend or ignore acts of Congress, and to play judge, jury, and jailer of individuals he deemed a threat to the state.

It falls now to the American people to pressure Congress, candidates for president, and future presidents to reverse the precedents set by the Bush administration, lest they lay the foundation for another president pursuing yet another twisted version of the U.S. Constitution. Nothing less than a new civic understanding about the limits of the war powers is now required to demonstrate that Americans take the Constitution seriously. The movement should be broad, bipartisan, and decoupled from any issue or any cause, in recognition that a president who invokes war powers to take away liberty can take away your religious freedom, your right to free speech, or, if you like, your gun.

As a first step, the commander in chief clause must be restored to its proper context within the framework of the Constitution. Article II assigns to the president the role of commander in chief of the U.S. Army and U.S. Navy, not commander in chief of war. Article I grants Congress ten explicit responsibilities associated with war, including the power to declare war. The shared authority reflects the overall scheme of checks and balances designed to ensure limited government. Checks and balances stand as the "interior structure" of the Constitution, Madison said, without which nothing else makes sense. These arrangements are not divisions of labor, as the modern arguments seem to suggest, or the stuff of a managerial flow chart premised on efficiency or avoidance of "micromanagement," but rather attempts to reconcile robust leadership with robust liberty. The war powers especially implicate liberty, as several of the framers said during the debates in Philadelphia, not only because of the serious consequences of war but because of the potential they offer for executive self-aggrandizement, particularly in the presence of a standing army. That was why war especially was a joint responsibility of the executive and legislative branches.

Bush did not act alone. The legislative branch repeatedly shirked its responsibility by approving broad authorizations to use military force that amounted to blank checks and standing by as the president cashed them in. In its lassitude, Congress continued a long tradition. Out of thirteen extended wars fought by the United States in the twentieth century, only two, World Wars I and II, were declared by Congress. By its passivity, Congress has consigned itself to a peripheral role never intended by the Constitution. Worse still, its acquiescence has served to bolster the administration's legal arguments for overreaching authority. Since the Supreme Court rarely intervenes in disputes between the elected branches, their practices tend to take on their own weight as legal precedents. Congress's inactivity, indeed, is the main pillar of the Bush administration's claims of sole authority over war (and everything remotely related to war). In its briefs and memoranda on war powers, eavesdropping, torture, and detention, an administration claiming fidelity to the "original intent" of the framers relied largely on Congress's historical noninvolvement rather than on anything the framers did. Distilled to its essence, the Bush administration argument is that whatever the framers meant, and whatever the Constitution says, it has all been rendered irrelevant by Congress's tolerance for unilateral presidential war making, which is tantamount to a waiver by Congress, never mind that the Constitution is not Congress's to waive.

Would the public or the Congress tolerate, say, the imposition of taxes by the president on his or her own? If not, why are they so accepting of the president's assumption of war powers meant to be shared? The answer needs some careful scholarly study, but surely it has something to do with intolerance of dissent in wartime and a misplaced notion of the patriotic thing to do when confronting the enemy. But if dispensation seems patriotic in a prewar state, then the definition of patriotism must be broadened to include maintenance of our basic form of limited government. A narrower definition invites exploitation.

Long before September 11, 2001, the neoconservative movement convinced itself that Congress had dangerously eroded presidential power in overreaction to the abuses of Vietnam and Watergate. As far back as 1976, neoconservative patriarchs such as Norman Podhoretz were writing that a liberal "attack on the powers of the presidency" was hindering the war on communism.[1] With 9/11, a new generation of neoconservatives seized upon a new war—the war on terrorism—to reverse the pendulum. Leading the charge was Vice President Dick Cheney, declaring restoration of executive power his solemn "obligation." In thirty-four years, he said in 2002, "I have repeatedly seen an erosion of the powers and the ability of the president of the United States to do his job.... And one of the things that I feel an obligation and I know the president does too, because we talked about it, is to pass on our offices in better shape than we found them to our successors. We are weaker today as an institution because of the unwise compromises that have been made over the last 30 to 35 years."[2]

In line with this agenda, Bush-Cheney administration lawyers would make the following breathtaking assertions:

- That it is the right and duty of the president to say what the Constitution means insofar as it concerns the core prerogatives of president.

- That, having said what the Constitution means, any contrary action by any other branch of government is presumptively unconstitutional and therefore null and void.
- That, since the war power is a core prerogative, its exercise by the president is beyond congressional regulation.

The administration thus claimed total control over war and all matters related to war, including defining the battlefield as a global battlefield that expressly encompassed U.S. soil. ("We are the battlefield," Bush declared in 2002, in a comment that seemed then a mere rhetorical flourish.) If the battlefield is global, then extraordinary war powers reserved for the battle-field may be applied anywhere, in justification of kidnapping, detention, eavesdropping, and "alternative means of interrogation" such as torture.

Here is how it sounded in administration legalese: "The Executive Branch uniformly has construed the Commander in Chief and foreign affairs powers to grant the President authority that is beyond the ability of Congress to regulate," the Justice Department said in support of illegal eavesdropping. It continued: "The extent of the President's Commander in Chief authority necessarily depends on where the enemy is found and where the battle is waged." In the present conflict, it added, "the battlefield was brought to the United States in the most literal way, and the United States continues to face a threat of further attacks on its soil."[3]

All of which takes us back to the framers' concern about a president assuming monarchic power and how much easier it is to do so citing the war powers rather than, say, the appointment power. If one disagrees with an application of the appointment power, one cannot be accused of giving comfort to the enemy.

It is jarring to hear of monarchic pretensions by a president of the United States. Yet after nearly two terms of the Bush administration, such references are no longer all that controversial. "Especially since 9/11, the executive branch has chronically usurped legislative or judicial power, and has repeatedly claimed that the President is the law," said a call for action from four prominent conservatives in Washington, D.C., Bruce Fein, David Keene, Bob Barr, and Richard Viguerie. "The constitutional grievances against the White House are chilling, reminiscent of the kingly abuses that provoked the Declaration of Independence."[4]

Elizabeth Drew, writing of Bush's "Power Grab" in the New York Review of Books, quoted Republican strategist Grover Norquist as saying: "If you interpret the Constitution's saying that the president is commander in chief to mean that the president can do anything he wants and can ignore the laws, you don't have a constitution: you have a king.... They're not trying to change the law; they're saying that they're above the law and in the case of the NSA wiretaps they break it."[5]

A study by the libertarian Cato Institute in January 2005 said this: "Unfortunately, far from defending the Constitution, President Bush has repeatedly sought to strip out the limits the document places on federal power. In its official legal briefs and public actions, the Bush administration has advanced a view of federal power that is astonishingly broad [and] sharply at odds with the text, history, and structure of our Constitution, which authorizes a government of limited powers."

The American Bar Association, not easily provoked, had this to say about presidential signing statements: Article II, Section 3 of the Constitution says "that the President shall take care that the laws be faithfully executed.... Because the 'take care' obligation of the President requires him to faithfully execute all laws, his obligation is to veto bills he believes are unconstitutional. He may not sign them into law and then emulate King James II by refusing to enforce them. In particular, the Framers sought to prevent in our new government the abuses that had arisen from the exercise of prerogative power by the Crown. Their device for doing so was to vest lawmaking power in the Congress and enforcement power in the President."[6]

And this from the Supreme Court justice Bush has described as a model justice: The founders, wrote Justice Antonin Scalia in dissent in the detention case of *Hamdi vs. Rumsfeld,* had a

general mistrust of military power permanently at the Executive's disposal. Except for the actual command of military forces, all authorization for their maintenance and all explicit authorization for their use is placed in the control of Congress under Article I, rather than the President under Article II. As Hamilton explained, the President's military authority would be "much inferior" to that of the British King.... A view of the Constitution that gives the Executive authority to use military force rather than the force of law against citizens on American soil flies in the face of the mistrust that engendered these provisions....

The Founders well understood the difficult tradeoff between safety and freedom," Scalia said. They "warned us about the risk, and equipped us with a Constitution designed to deal with it. Many think it not only inevitable but entirely proper that liberty give way to security in times of national crisis—that, at the extremes of military exigency, inter arma silent leges. Whatever the general merits of the view that war silences law or modulates its voice, that view has no place in the interpretation and application of a Constitution designed precisely to confront war and, in a manner that accords with democratic principles, to accommodate it."[7]

The public and the news media must now extract commitments from candidates for president and Congress to restore the checks and balances demanded by the Constitution. Candidates must be confronted with the Bush administration's claims of power and explicitly asked whether they agree, for example, that the president is empowered under any circumstances to override laws, and whether they agree or disagree that a president can order the indefinite detention of citizens and noncitizens alike without due process and, if so, under what circumstances.

Americans must insist that our public servants take seriously their oaths to support and defend the Constitution—the Constitution we have.

Notes

1. Norman Podhoretz, "Making the World Safe for Communism," *Commentary*, 61:4 (April 1976) p. 34.

2. Dick Cheney, interview with Sam Donaldson and Cokie Roberts on ABC's *This Week*, January 27, 2002.

3. "Legal Authorities Supporting the Activities of the National Security Agency Described by the President," Department of Justice White Paper, released January 19, 2006.

4. Open Letter to the President by the American Freedom Agenda, April 2007.

5. June 22, 2006.

6. American Bar Association, *Report of the Task Force on Presidential Signing Statements and Separation of Powers Doctrine*, August 2006.

7. Dissent in *Hamdi v. Rumsfeld*, June 28, 2004.

Chapter 13

Torture No More

Aziz Huq

"Stuff Happens"

Too often, human beings like to hurt each other. In the 1960s, empirical work by American psychologists Philip G. Zimbardo and Stanley Milgram demonstrated that ordinary individuals, given apparent authority or permission, will inflict pain even unto death. In these experiments, Zimbardo and Milgram gestured to a psychological undercurrent that set torture apart from other atrocities of war. Unlike the twentieth century's other symphonic horrors of the battlefield—chemical warfare, carpet bombing, cluster mining—torture operates on an intrinsically interpersonal level: Torture cannot be conducted from 50,000 feet.

Torture, under governing international and domestic legal rules, is limited in most circumstances to state action. But in today's sprawling military and intelligence bureaucracies, the grip that torture has on the human psyche gives it special virulence. Torture, when licensed implicitly or explicitly, spreads in institutions as more and more people find within themselves the urge to dominate other human beings. As a result, torture is hard to rein in.

Rooting out torture is more difficult than addressing many other kinds of human rights violations because the spaces of torture—police interrogation rooms, forward operating bases in Iraq, or Central Intelligence Agency (CIA) prisons around the world—lie beyond the ken of ordinary judicial or democratic control. Torture appears in sites already swathed in darkness, where constitutional and administrative constraints are weakest. After the fact, false accusations are hard to sift from legitimate complaints.

Nor are democracies immune from torture. To the contrary, torture has been endemic to liberal democracies, where it has long been used to entrench boundaries of social, class, and especially racial stratification. Liberal democracies use the rack and screw, or their modern descendants, to keep the inhabitants of the ghetto and the colony in their place. Torture thus haunts the jails of colonial East Asia and North Africa, the barracks of Londonderry, and the police stations of Chicago's South Side, implicitly licensed by democracies for use against those who have (in Joseph Conrad's pungent phrase) "a different complexion or slightly flatter noses than ourselves."[1] That torture would be used today against those with a different skin color, a different faith, and a different passport from most Americans ought not to surprise. Today's torture is merely the persistence of old pathologies in new, pernicious forms.

Yet today's problem seems different in scale and intensity. Between 2004 and today, the contours of a regularized set of protocols on torture—sexual and religious humiliation, "stress positions," "environmental manipulation," and more—have emerged. Evidence of these practices has accreted from Iraq, Guantánamo Bay, and the CIA's clandestine prisons scattered around the globe from Thailand to Morocco. While protesting that it does not use torture, the Bush administration has vigorously opposed legislation or regulation that would prohibit or criminalize these methods. In 2006, it secured a rollback of criminal liability from Congress. Then, in July 2007, Bush issued a presidential order for the CIA that, among other things, eliminated sleep deprivation from the prohibition on illegal coercion. Vice President Cheney has made no secret of his enthusiasm for waterboarding. So it is too late in the day to claim that torture is not state policy under President Bush. Attempting to reverse that policy demands some understanding of how it began.

How We Torture

On April 28, 2004, CBS broadcast the first photographs of abuse at Abu Ghraib. The Abu Ghraib photos were not the first evidence of abuse to surface. Previously, the International Committee of the Red Cross had issued numerous reports to the military warning of abuse; the military responded by trying to curtail Red Cross access to Iraqi prisons.

From the pictures' first broadcast, the administration blamed "bad apples." On May 7, 2004, Secretary of Defense Donald Rumsfeld told the Senate and House Armed Services Committees that "these terrible acts were perpetrated by a small number of the U.S. military," and that "the President didn't know . . . I didn't know." Official reports about Abu Ghraib and detainee treatment also toed this line. The army inspector general's report on Abu Ghraib, for example, concluded that the "abuses, while regrettable, are aberrations."

But the photographed antics of the 800th Military Police Brigade, stationed at the Abu Ghraib prison in late 2003, were not "aberrational," except in one limited sense: Most U.S. torture was not mere amorphous and extracurricular sadism akin to the Abu Ghraib incidents. Rather, the overwhelming volume of torture in Iraq, Guantánamo, and CIA prisons occurred in structured interrogations, rigidly directed by protocol approved by senior civilian personnel, and deliberately applied for the specific purpose of extracting information. In blaming "bad apples," the administration sought to obscure the generalized permission granted to abuse and the detailed protocols disseminated through the military and the CIA to license and facilitate that abuse.

The administration built a torture culture in three steps: First, there was an assault on the law against torture. Second came veiled but unequivocal commands to use coercion and torture in a context that made endemic abuse inevitable. And finally, there was a systematic evisceration of oversight mechanisms used to deter torture. I will consider each of these steps in turn.

In January 2002, the White House, and specifically Vice President Richard Cheney, decided to adopt "robust interrogation" measures. To this end, the first step was to change the law. The United States once had clear laws against torture, including a federal criminal statute that categorically prohibited torture; the international Convention Against Torture and Other Cruel, Inhuman, and Degrading Treatment or Punishment[2]; and the 1949 Geneva Conventions covering the treatment of wartime detainees, which prohibit not only torture but also "humiliating and degrading treatment." In a legalistic, bureaucratic culture, the prospect of liability under these laws would at least slow efforts to adopt torture qua policy.

So without telling Congress or the American people, the White House changed the law. On February 7, 2002, President George W. Bush, apparently at his vice president's urging, signed an executive order abrogating the Geneva Conventions' protections for prisoners captured in Afghanistan or linked to al-Qaeda. Instead, Bush stipulated, the military would treat prisoners "humanely" unless military necessity required otherwise. The order said nothing about the CIA, which did not even have to honor the vague "humanely" standard. Further, as administration officials Timothy Flanigan and Alberto Gonzales have testified, the "humanely" standard lacked any precise meaning: It depended wholly on contextual factors. In the administration's Orwellian view, in the right context any tactic could be construed as "humane." Administration rhetoric categorically treating detainees as evil beyond redemption also made it more likely that individual officials would assume the circumstances justified extreme coercion.

Having eviscerated the Geneva Conventions, the administration still needed to undo the domestic criminal law against torture. Its action in this area involved two separate legal opinions for the CIA and the military, issued by the Justice Department in August 2002 and March 2003, respectively. These rulings demolished almost every legal restraint on torture. The former posited that only pain analogous to organ failure counted as torture. Under that definition, when the president proclaimed that the United States didn't torture, he was misleadingly using words in a way that no one else would understand.

The second step toward a torture culture involved high-ranking officials giving endorsement to torture. The command came early and from on high. In early 2002, Secretary of Defense Donald Rumsfeld took a personal interest in the treatment of one Saudi detainee at Guantánamo, Mohamed al-Qahtani, whose interrogation thereafter included sleep deprivation, forced nudity, sexual humiliation, and the use of dogs to assault. Rumsfeld also sanctioned the use of coercive measures against the broader inmate population at Guantánamo. Then in late 2003, he dispatched General Geoffrey Miller from his command at Guantánamo to advise U.S. jailors on how to "Gitmoize Iraq."[3] The result, former Iraq interrogators confirm, was the muddying of Geneva's application in Iraq. As former defense secretary James Schlesinger concluded, "Policies approved for use on al Qaeda and Taliban detainees who were not afforded the protection of [enemy prisoner of war] status under the Geneva Conventions now applied to detainees who did fall under the Geneva Convention protections." In stages, the civilian leadership deliberately pushed not only the CIA but also the military into abusive interrogations.

Midlevel commanders took the hint. An email from an army captain in Iraq obtained by the American Civil Liberties Union, for example, reported that: "Col[onel] Boltz has made it clear that we want these individuals broken. Casualties are mounting and we need to start gathering info."[4] In the words of the army's inspector general, senior military and civilian leaders fostered a "do what it takes mindset" and "encouraged behavior at the harsher end of the acceptable range of behavior toward detainees."[5]

White House leadership, or its absence, mattered in another regard: by planning a war and setting goals in a way that made endemic abuse certain. Torture's spread in the Iraq theater must be seen as a corollary of the overarching failure—amply documented elsewhere in this volume—to plan and provide resources for postinvasion scenarios. Failure to manage the postinvasion period hastened the insurgency, which in turn yielded tremendous pressure for "actionable" intelligence. The absence of counterinsurgency know-how then led to mass roundups and indiscriminate seizure that overwhelmed the detention system and precipitated abuse. According to Major General George Fay, who investigated Abu Ghraib, "Large quantities of detainees with little or no intelligence value swelled Abu Ghraib's population.... Already scarce interrogator and analyst resources were pulled from interrogations operations to identify and screen" new detainees, and the absence of appropriate procedures meant few were released. Amid growing, unexpected violence and no resources to deal with it, the potential for torture and abuse was plentiful.

As a consequence, reports of abuse came not only from Baghdad prisons such as Abu Ghraib and Camp Cropper, but also from forward operating bases around Iraq and from bases in Afghanistan and Guantánamo. Common patterns emerged of similar techniques of systematic psychological coercion and physical manipulation, techniques first refined by a Pentagon program called "Survival, Evasion, Resistance, and Escape" (SERE), that was developed after the Korean War to train pilots to resist enemy torture.

Yet—and this is the third and final part of the conscious effort to cultivate torture—only a handful of incidents were investigated, and almost no prosecutions ensued. The federal government has a panoply of tools to ensure accountability, even aside from judicial and congressional investigations. They include internal audits, the inspectors general system established in 1977, special prosecutors, and criminal prosecutions. Yet, as Human Rights First concluded, there were "failures to investigate all relevant agencies and personnel; cumulative reporting (increasing the risk that errors and omissions may be perpetuated in successive reports); contradictory conclusions; questionable use of security classification to withhold information; failure to address senior military and civilian command responsibility; and, perhaps, above all, the absence of any clear plan for corrective action." In addition, investigators earned no glory for their labors. On the contrary, General Antonio Taguba, who first investigated Abu Ghraib, was told, "You and your report will be investigated."[6] It is thus no accident that accountability started and stopped at the bottom of the barrel: Any effort to go farther was swiftly stopped.

Stopping Torture

No law, no leadership, and no sunlight. Under such conditions, the impulse toward abuse was bound to flourish, as the experience in Iraq makes clear. Once it has, the question is how to stamp it out. Torture may not be wholly eliminated, but it can be reduced. A tripartite strategy, echoing the administration's flaws, is required that involves law, leadership, and sunlight.

Start with the law. In September 2006, the administration secured legislation, the Military Commissions Act, that both muddied the scope of Geneva protection and undermined the strength of criminal sanctions under the 1996 War Crimes Act. After the former law was passed, the kind of torture carried out in Iraq may be even harder to prevent in the future. Moreover, it seems that the White House has not fully retreated from the otiose definition of torture first articulated in the August 2002 Department of Justice "torture memo." Absent legal clarity, however, practical change is unlikely. Law not only sets enforceable bounds but also enunciates shared ethical commitments. Knowing that an act is unlawful has a restraining effect on government agents. Congress and the White House must restore the U.S. commitment against torture by reaffirming the nation's commitment to the Geneva Conventions and to the minimal standards of Article III in that document. Further, the Justice Department must renounce its pinched definition of torture and promulgate a clear definition that applies both to the military and the CIA.

Then there is the question of leadership. The White House has failed on this count. Others, such as former Senator Zell Miller of Georgia, who derided critics of the Abu Ghraib abuses for "rushing to give aid and comfort to the enemy," have shown callous disregard for the facts (most of those detained at Abu Ghraib, the military conceded, were wrongly held)[7]; they have managed to compound the harm to the reputation of the United States in their rush to reap political gain.

But torture should be a matter beyond politics. To reinforce clear laws, an unequivocal message that torture is unacceptable and never necessary is required. On this point, the military leadership is far ahead of its civilian cohort. In May 2007, General David H. Petraeus sent a letter to troops warning that "expedient methods" using force violated American values and would not be tolerated.

Present conditions in Iraq make the need for leadership especially pressing. A May 2007 Pentagon report indicated that fewer than half the U.S. soldiers now stationed in Iraq would report abuse. Ever-increasing deployment durations strain troops in ways that make abuse more likely. Further, torture rates will likely spike as the ill-trained, brutal, and sectarian Iraqi army "steps up." Even in the event of a rapid drawdown of U.S. forces in Iraq, the United States would have to plan for and respond to the acceleration of abuse by its allies.

Finally, there is what Supreme Court justice Louis Brandeis called the "best disinfectant": sunlight.[8] To reestablish the moral standing of the United States, a thorough investigation of abuse, torture, and detainee deaths in military and CIA custody is needed. Existing oversight mechanisms have been stymied, suggesting the need for installation of markedly more aggressive measures, including a special military prosecutor. Moving forward, measures as simple as digitally recording interrogations are needed. Such rules must be accompanied by strong protections for rank-and-file whistle-blowers and also senior personnel, such as General Taguba, who investigate torture.

To fight against the kind of torture perpetrated in Iraq in these ways is to set the nation's face against a strain in human nature that cannot be eliminated, only mitigated. So these measures—law, leadership, and sunlight—will not wholly end torture. They will, however, mitigate its occurrence. In an imperfect world that may be aspiration enough for now.

Notes

1. Joseph Conrad, *Heart of Darkness* (London: Penguin Press, 1995) pp.31–32.

2. The convention was adopted on December 10, 1984, and is contained in full in S. Treaty Document No. 100-20 (1988).

3. Frederick A. O. Schwartz and Aziz Z. Huq, *Unchecked and Unbalanced: Presidential Power in a Time of Terror* (New York: New Press, 2007), pp. 86–87.

4. Email from Captain William Ponce, available at www.pbs.org/wgbh/torture/paper/ponce.html.

5. Inspector General, U.S. Department of the Army, "Detainee Operations Inspection," July 21, 2004.

6. Human Rights First, "Getting to Ground Truth: U.S. Investigations in

the War Against Terror," available at http://www.humanrightsfirst.org/us_law/detainess/getting_to_ground_truth.htm; and Seymour Hersh, "The General's Report," *New Yorker,* June 25, 2006.

7. Sen. Zell Miller's statement on the Senate floor is posted at http://laughatliberals.com/blog/archives/2004/05/; For statements regarding the military's admission that most prisoners at Abu Ghraib were being wrongly held, see Mark Danner, "Abu Ghraib: The Hidden Story," *New York Review of Books,* October 7, 2004.

8. Brandies, Louis Dembitz, *Other People's Money, and How the Banks Use It* (New York: Frederick A. Stokes, 1932).

Chapter 14

The Shadow Army

Privatization

Janine R. Wedel

To an extent unknown to most Americans, the U.S. occupation of Iraq has been managed by a huge shadow army of private contractors. All too often this army has been uncommandable and unaccountable, its interests dangerously divergent from those of the government it ostensibly serves.

The Bush administration came into office bent on privatizing as many government functions as possible, according to the conviction that in most realms, the private sector is likely to do a better job.

The result of that, as well as a long process of contracting out, is a war run with the massive participation of private companies. As of July 2007, U.S.-paid contractors "serving" in Iraq outnumbered U.S. troops. Some

160,000 soldiers plus several thousand U.S. civilian employees rely greatly on the 180,000 U.S.-funded contractors,[1] of which some 21,000 were Americans (about 43,000 foreign contractors and 118,000 Iraqis made up the rest).[2] This is despite President Bush's "surge" that began in January 2007, which added nearly 30,000 soldiers and support units.

The record-breaking use of private contractors conceals from public view many of the true demands and costs of the war, among them the manpower required and casualties exacted. Behind the façade, public and private soldiers are treated differently. No flags are waved, nor are parades staged, when contractors come marching home. They are not included in U.S. casualty figures or tracked by any single U.S. agency. As of the end of June 2007, 1,001 U.S.-funded contractors had lost their lives in Iraq, in addition to the 3,561 deaths of military personnel.

The heavy dependence on private contractors in the military is new; the war in Iraq has been the most privatized in U.S. history. In the 1991 Gulf War, only 9,200 contractors supported 540,000 military personnel. The Defense Department is the federal government's biggest buyer of services. In fiscal year 2006 the department obligated upward of $151 billion to service contracts, an increase since fiscal year 1996 of 78 percent.[3]

The virtual transfer of many military functions to the private sector has occurred at the same time that government oversight, and the capacity for it, has diminished. The Department of Defense is ever more dependent on contractors to supply a host of "mission-critical services," according to the U.S. Government Accountability Office (GAO). These services include information technology systems, interpreters, and intelligence analysts, as well as weapons system maintenance and base operation support."[4] And, today, not only such services, but also functions that were once the responsibility of military personnel, along with entirely new portfolios, are now essentially in private hands.

For instance, contractors do the following:

- Draft official documents. Websites of contractors working for the Department of Defense have posted announcements of job openings for analysts to perform such functions as preparing the Defense Department budget. One contractor boasted of having written the Army's Field Manual on "Contractors on the Battlefield."[5]
- Choose other contractors. The Pentagon has employed contractors to counsel it on selecting other contractors.[6]
- Perform most information technology (IT) work: Contractors were doing more than three-quarters of the federal government's IT work, even before the war-related major push to contract out.[7] Information

technology is a critical force behind contemporary military operations.

Yet, while private companies are acquiring government functions and the
number of contractors is on the rise, the number of Defense Department
employees available to oversee them has declined.[8] For fifteen years, the
GAO has included the Pentagon's contract management operation on its list
of "high-risk" activities. This designation means that the department may
well lack "the ability to effectively manage cost, quality and performance in
contracts," according to U.S. comptroller general David M. Walker, head
of the GAO.[9] When these deficiencies play out on the ground in Iraq, they
can have serious consequences. In 2006 the GAO found that "problems
with management and oversight of contractors have negatively impacted
military operations and unit morale and hindered DOD's ability to obtain
reasonable assurance that contractors are effectively meeting their contract
requirements in the most cost-efficient manner."[10]

The extensive transfer of functions to the private sector raises even more
fundamental concerns. The overarching goal of government is supposedly
the adoption of policies and practices that promote the public good. For
contractors performing government services, the bottom line is profit.
A book by investigative reporter Dana Rasor and criminal investigator
Robert Bauman is replete with examples of how contractors are pulled by
incentives that differ from those of the military, thus negatively impacting
their reliability and performance on the battlefield. Some contractors have
delayed the fulfillment of their commitments without consequence. Some
have walked away.[11]

Further, military personnel are governed by regulations that do not apply to contractors. They do not fall under the rules of war or the Geneva
Convention. The records of private employees in war zones are exempt
from scrutiny under the Freedom of Information Act, which applies only
to "agency" records. And, unlike military personnel, contract employees
on the battlefield can quit their jobs without fear of penalty under the
Uniform Code of Military Justice, though, of course, their employers are
free to fire them.

Another damaging effect of privatization reflected in the Iraq war stems
from changes instituted under the Clinton administration's "reinventing
government" effort. While that administration introduced "reforms" in
procurement procedures, Clinton's successor intensified the process, throw-
ing billions more dollars into the mix. A top government procurement
official whose tenure spanned the administrations of George H. W. Bush,
Bill Clinton, and George W. Bush put it succinctly: "Clinton laid the

framework and set the speed limit at 500 miles per hour but never drove the car past 250. Bush tested the limit."

The Clinton initiative transformed government contracting rules with regard to oversight, transparency, and competition. The procurement process was streamlined, ostensibly to make it more efficient. As a result, since the 1990s, small contracts often have been replaced by bigger, and frequently open-ended, multiyear, multi-million-dollar, and even multi-billion-dollar contracts. The changes may, in part, have simplified bureaucracy, but they certainly introduced much greater subjectivity into the process of awarding contracts. Federal officials can now select the contractors they want to do the work, rather than going through the traditional bidding system. That change enables much more discretion on the part of those who award contracts and, therefore, increases their ability to make decisions based on personal networks. Thus who you know—and who you owe—are more likely to become determining factors in contract decisions.

Nearly all contractors working in Iraq are doing so under what is known as indefinite delivery/indefinite quantity contracts (ID/IQs). The awarding of these contracts includes a competitive process. However, they are not contracts in the traditional sense, but rather agreements to do business in the future—with the price and scope of work to be determined. Despite the legal fiction of "full and open competition," in practice, the names of pre-approved contractors appear on a list, which confers on them preferred vendor status. A government agency maintains the list, to which that agency and, usually other agencies, can turn to buy everything ranging from pens to contractors' services. Program officials and contracting officers select contractors from the list for specific jobs.

A company's inclusion on the list provides what has been called a "hunting license" because once they are on the list, those favored contractors can then lobby government officials for specific work tasks.

The ID/IQ contracts create conditions under which unclear lines of authority and a lack of accountability can thrive. Although ID/IQ contracts can reduce the time, costs, and bureaucracy incurred in separate purchases, these larger, often open-ended, and potentially much more lucrative contracts are much more likely to diffuse authority and responsibility.

Although ID/IQ contracts are supposed to enhance efficiency by putting suppliers in place whose services can be readily accessed, the reality is that favored contractors make the list, at least in some cases, because of their personal connections with the government officials. Huge, noncompetitive awards, justified on national security grounds, have been granted for work in Iraq. Defense companies linked to senior members of the administration's inner circles have been the beneficiaries of some of these awards. Audits conducted by the inspectors general for the Departments of Defense and Interior (which manages some Defense contracts in exchange for payment) found that more than half the contracts inspected were granted without competition or without checking to see that the prices were sensible.[12] Thus, even as government has been drained of its oversight capability, business competition—the key to cost savings—has diminished.

Some of these contracts have had disastrous consequences. CACI, the Arlington, Virginia–based company, some of whose employees were among those involved in the Abu Ghraib prisoner abuse scandal in Iraq, were working under such a contract. The scandal highlights the complications surrounding these contracts. First, ID/IQ contractors such as CACI are not legally authorized to sell goods or services not provided for in their contract. Yet that rule is often breached. The inspector general of the Department of the Interior (which was legally responsible for CACI but had little capacity to monitor it) and the General Services Administration (the government agency that manages government properties and purchasing) found, after the scandal broke in the media, that the contract under which CACI supplied interrogators was an IT contract; it was not approved to provide interrogation services.[13]

A second troublesome practice promoted by ID/IQ contracts is that they augment the discretionary authority of government officials whose entities require the services of contractors. When the Defense Department needed personnel, CACI, which had a long collaboration with the department, was well positioned to supply them. CACI officials told GAO investigators that they "marketed their services directly to Army intelligence and logistics officials in Iraq because of relationships they had developed over time."[14]

To make matters worse, the dearth of manpower and expertise in government that has resulted from caps on or reductions in the number of civil servants may encourage contractors to take advantage of lax participation on the part of government officials. GAO determined that CACI "effectively replaced government decision-makers in several aspects of the procurement process."[15]

Although the Defense Department enlisted the services of CACI, authority did not flow from Defense to CACI. That highlights a third widespread practice common with ID/IQs: The entity with the demand for the contractor—and with whom the contractor will work most closely—is neither necessarily the legal contracting entity nor legally responsible for monitoring the contractor. The result is that, in many cases, it is difficult to speak of a chain of command, even a convoluted one. CACI's work was for the Defense Department, but Defense relied on the Interior Department to issue individual task orders (a kind of minicontract that specifies particular work assignments) and to manage the contract—an interagency arrangement made possible (and very common) through the changes in the procurement system discussed above.[16] Although the Interior Department was legally responsible for CACI, Interior lacked the capacity to gather information about or monitor CACI's Iraq activities.

In broad terms, then, military commanders are supposedly responsible for the conduct of contractors working in the war effort. Yet, as became clear in the CACI case, once contracts are let, the same formal operational control that would apply through a government chain of command does not necessarily apply to contractors. One result, clearly, is the obfuscation of authority. And, with much of the work in Iraq done under ID/IQ contracts, CACI is unlikely to be an aberrant case.

The current procurement system thus erodes the hallmark accountability of government while also impairing what is supposed to be the defining feature of business: competition. It also enables a new culture of ambiguity and leaves unclear just who is minding the store. Even *before* the war in Iraq, in April 2002, the army reported to Congress that its best guess was that it directly or indirectly employed between 124,000 and 605,000 service contract workers—a discrepancy of half a million workers.[17] Such vacuums of authority and information offer a golden opportunity for private individuals and coordinated networks to seize command of policy, business, and national destiny in pursuit of their own interests.

The Iraq war has exposed the dangers of contracting out vital state functions to private actors. Such massive privatization renders government more susceptible to the influence of unelected private players with their own interests—players who are far removed from the oversight of government and scrutiny of voters.

Inherently governmental functions, such as the direction of military and intelligence operations, should not be privatized. It is vital to reverse Clinton-era procurement "reforms" and to restore effective government oversight. It is also necessary to depress the aggressive enactment of those reforms on the part of any administration. As long as the United States continues to contract out critical government functions, the public can be more easily misled, and U.S. interests, along with its moral standing, will be repeatedly undercut by a shadow army.

Notes

1. T. Christian Miller, "Private Contractors Outnumber U.S. Troops in Iraq," *Los Angeles Times,* July 4, 2007, http://www.latimes.com/news/nationworld/nation/la-na-private4jul04,1,7664713,full.story?coll=la-headlines-nation (accessed 7/05/2007). The article states that these figures may underrepresent private security contractors.

2. T. Christian Miller, "Private Contractors Outnumber U.S. Troops in Iraq," *Los Angeles Times,* July 4, 2007.

3. GAO, Statement of John P. Hutton, Director, Acquisition and Sourcing Management; Testimony Before the Subcommittee on Defense, Committee on Appropriations, House of Representatives. *Defense Acquisitions: Improved Management and Oversight Needed to Better Control DOD's Acquisition of Services,* Washington, DC, GAO-07-832T.

4. Testimony of John P. Hutton, acting director, Acquisition and Sourcing Management, Government Accountability Office, "Hearing of the Defense Subcommittee of the House Appropriations Committee; Subject: Defense Contracting," May 10, 2007,

5. Dan Guttman, "The Shadow Pentagon: Private Contractors Play a Huge Role in Basic Government Work—Mostly Out of Public View" (Washington, DC: Center for Public Integrity), September 29, 2004, http://www.publicintegrity.org/pns/printer-friendly.aspx?aid=386; see also: Headquarters: Department of the Army, "Contractors on the Battlefield," Field Manual No. 3-100.21, Washington, DC, 3 January 2003.

6. Larry Makinson, "Outsourcing the Pentagon: Who Benefits from the Politics and Economics of National Security?" (Washington, DC: Center for Public Integrity), September 29, 2004, p. 4, http://www.publicintegrity.org/pns/printer-friendly.aspx?aid=385.

7. According to the market research firm Input in Chantilly, Virginia ("Experiences Give and Take," *Government Executive,* July 1, 2003, www.govexec.com/feature/0603/ots03s4.htm (accessed 8/7/2007)).

8. Testimony of John P. Hutton, p. 2.

9. Comptroller General David Walker, Remarks at the George Washington University Law School Symposium on the Future of Competitive Sourcing, September 15, 2003, (transcript on file with *Public Contract Law Journal*).

10. GAO, "Military Operations: High-Level DOD Action Needed to Address Long-Standing Problems with Management and Oversight of Contractors Supporting Deployed Forces," United States Government Accountability Office, GAO-07-145, December 2006, p. 35.

11. Dana Rasor and Robert Bauman, *Betraying Our Troops: The Destructive Results of Privatizing War* (New York: Palgrave Macmillan), 2007.

12. Robert O'Harrow Jr. and Scott Higham, "Interior, Pentagon Faulted in Audits: Effort to Speed Defense Contracts Wasted Millions," *Washington Post,* December 25, 2006, p. A1.

13. GAO, "Interagency Contracting: Problems with DOD's and Interior's Orders to Support Military Operations," U.S. Government Accountability Office, GAO–05–201, April 2005, p. 7.

14. Ibid., p. 14.

15. Ibid.

16. Ibid.

17. Reported in Dan Guttman, "The Shadow Pentagon."

Chapter 15

Invitation to Steal

War Profiteering in Iraq

William D. Hartung

The heavy reliance on private contractors to do everything from serving meals and doing laundry to protecting oil pipelines and interrogating prisoners has been a major factor in the immense costs of the Iraq war. As of July 2007, there were more employees of private firms and their subcontractors on the ground in Iraq than there were U.S. military personnel.

One of the main rationales for using private companies to carry out functions formerly done by uniformed military personnel—a practice that has been on the rise since then Defense Secretary Dick Cheney commissioned a study that led to the contracting out of all army logistics work to Halliburton in the 1990s—was that it would save money. But in Iraq, the combination of greedy contractors and lax government oversight has resulted in exorbitant costs, many of them for projects that were never completed.

The first sign that something was terribly wrong with the contracting process for the war was the awarding of a no-bid, cost-plus contract to Halliburton, allegedly to pay the cost of putting out oil fires in Iraq. Representative Henry Waxman started asking questions about the contract after he learned that it could be worth up to $7 billion over two years. He rightly questioned how a no-bid deal justified on the basis of potential short-term emergencies could have such a long duration at such a high price. Only then was it revealed that the contract also covered the task of *operating* Iraq's oil infrastructure. Given the long-term nature of this larger task, Waxman argued that this aspect of the work be taken away from Halliburton and subjected to competitive bidding. It was several years before his recommendation was implemented, and even then Halliburton received what at least one potential competitor—Bechtel—viewed as an unfair advantage.

Even though few contracts matched the size of Halliburton's oil deal, the use of cost-plus awards was widely emulated. A cost-plus award is virtually an invitation to pad costs, as profits are a percentage of funds spent—in other words, the more you spend, the more you make. This problem has been compounded by a lack of auditors to scrutinize these contracts. For example, in one zone of Iraq, only eight people were assigned to oversee contracts worth over $2.5 billion.

Halliburton's other major contract in Iraq was for the Logistics Civil Augmentation Program (LOGCAP), carried out by its Kellogg, Brown, and Root subsidiary. Under this arrangement, Halliburton supplies virtually all the army's noncombat needs in the field, from building and operating bases to repairing and maintaining combat vehicles. LOGCAP operates on a variation of the cost-plus contract, and it has exploited this arrangement to the fullest. Among the overcharges engaged in by the company have been the following: overcharging by more than a dollar a gallon for fuel shipped into Iraq from Kuwait, billing the government for three times as many meals as it actually served the troops at several of the bases it runs, leasing sport utility vehicles for its personnel at a cost of $7,000 per month, and charging $100 each for doing a bag of laundry. These are just a few examples among dozens in which Halliburton took advantage of the "fog of war" to line its pockets. The company's attitude was summed up by company whistleblower Henry Bunting, who indicated that when he raised questions with his supervisor about Halliburton's lavish expenditures of government money, he was told "don't worry about it, it's cost-plus."[1]

In all, Halliburton has been by far the greatest beneficiary of the Iraq war, with war-related contracts exceeding $8 billion, several billion of which has not been adequately accounted for. Although a number of changes were made in response to the company's record of fraud and abuse—from taking away its fuel supply contract to splitting the work for operating Iraq's oil infrastructure into three parts—these measures were a classic case of too little, too late. Halliburton's subsequent spin-off of its Kellog, Brown, and Root subsidiary is unlikely to change the dynamic outlined thus far. Reforms designed to prevent "another Halliburton" will be discussed below.

Large firms like Halliburton were not the only ones to exploit the war for excess—and in some cases illegal—profits. One of the most notorious examples involved Custer Battles, named after its founders Scott Custer and Michael Battles. When the two men went to Iraq in search of contracts, they had no capital, no employees, and no experience in the security business. But they did have a knack for marketing, billing themselves "Green Berets with MBAs."

Shortly after arriving in Iraq, Custer Battles received a lucrative contract to provide security for the Baghdad airport. As an example of just how loose controls were, one early payment to the company was made in the form of $2 million in shrink-wrapped $20 bills, transferred to the firm in exchange for a handwritten receipt. A film of two Custer employees playing football with a brick of the shrink wrapped bills provided one of the most enduring images of greed and corruption generated by the Iraq occupation contracting fiasco.

Even as rumors of poor performance on the airport security contract began to circulate, Custer Battles received another major contract, this time for delivering the new Iraqi currency to key points around the country. This effort was characterized by shoddy working conditions, unpaid subcontractors, and the use of broken-down trucks that could not carry out their mission.

Finally, after revelations by whistle-blowers who had worked for the firm, the extent of Custer Battles's corruption was exposed. In addition to failing to provide the security and transport services it was contracted to do, internal company documents showed that it had routinely charged for at least twice the value of services supplied by padding bills and funneling subcontracts to phony companies. While all this was going on, Mike Battles was paying himself $3 million as head of the company.

These were far from isolated incidents, but the extent of the problem might never have been known without the creation of the position of special inspector general for Iraq reconstruction (SIGIR). Inspector General Stuart Bowen and his staff did scores of audits of every aspect of the reconstruction effort, from building schools to restoring electric service to providing security for a wide range of projects and activities. They discovered a pattern in which contract dollars were spent in full, although only a fraction of the promised work had been completed. Some of this gap can be accounted for by the violence and insecurity that was rampant in significant parts of Iraq from early on in the occupation, but it cannot begin to account for the shoddy performance of major and minor contractors alike.

To cite just one example of a company that was roundly criticized in SIGIR audits, the Parsons Corporation—the second-largest Iraq reconstruction contactor after Halliburton—is worthy of mention. The company completely botched or failed to deliver on hundreds of millions of dollars worth of contracts to build health clinics, fire stations, prisons, and a police academy. This misconduct not only wasted dollars but endangered the lives of U.S. soldiers by fostering resentment among Iraqi citizens.

The lack of accountability for contractors in Iraq has extended well beyond financial malfeasance. Interrogators and translators from Titan and CACI were allegedly involved in incidents of torture at the infamous Abu Ghraib prison, but no employees of these firms were ever subjected to legal proceedings. Private contractors in Iraq exist in a legal never-never land, subject neither to Iraqi law nor to the Uniform Code of Military Justice. The U.S. Extraterritorial Justice Act is supposed to cover cases like this one, but it has almost never been utilized, due to the difficulty of having a prosecutor based in the United States build a case regarding an incident or incidents that may occur thousands of miles away.

The existence of security contractors who operate outside the military chain of command also poses serious problems. For example, when four employees of the private security firm Blackwater were killed and tortured by a mob in Fallujah in April 2004, the U.S. military felt compelled to strike hard at the city in a punitive backlash that did much to accelerate the opposition to the U.S. occupation among ordinary Iraqis. If the job—accompanying a convoy of food and kitchen equipment on behalf of Regency Hotel and Hospitality, another U.S. contractor in Iraq—had been done by personnel within the military chain of command, they might never have been deployed to that location at that time, thereby preventing the first Fallujah crisis from ever occurring.[2]

Another circle of beneficiaries may be referred to as the "policy profiteers": individuals who advocated for the war with Iraq at the same time that they stood to gain from it. Chief among these were Bruce Jackson, R. James Woolsey, and Richard Perle. Jackson, a former vice president at the world's largest weapons contractor, Lockheed Martin, co-chaired the Committee for the Liberation of Iraq, an advocacy group that closely coordinated its pro-war messages with the Bush administration. He had previously served as chair of the foreign policy subcommittee of the Republican platform committee at the party's 2000 convention. Both Woolsey and Perle served as advisers to then Secretary of Defense Donald Rumsfeld as part of the Defense Policy Board. Both men used their posts as official advisers to the Pentagon to beat the drums for war, and both simultaneously ran investment funds that were receiving money from major contractors like Boeing that have profited mightily from the Iraq conflict. In addition, Woolsey is an executive at Booz, Allen, and Hamilton, a consulting firm that has given seminars on how to get Iraq-related contracts.

Preventing war profiteering on the scale that has prevailed in Iraq will require the implementation of thoroughgoing reforms:

- Increasing the use of competitive bidding, even in cases in which only a few contractors are deemed to be capable of doing the task at hand;
- Screening bidders more carefully to rule out companies with no experience in the relevant area of work (e.g., Custer Battles);
- Sending more auditors to the field from the outset of a conflict; and
- Setting up a new "Truman Committee," modeled on the effort by then Senator Harry Truman during World War II. The committee was authorized to inspect the facilities of war contractors, issue subpoenas to gather information, and bring criminal charges against companies engaged in defrauding the government. The committee should have subpoena power, a robust investigative staff, and the ability to forward major abuses to the relevant criminal authorities.

These initial steps would go a long way towards preventing fraud and misconduct in future conflicts.

Notes

1. Testimony of Henry Bunting, Senate Democratic Policy Committee, Hearing on Iraq Contracting Practices, February 13, 2004.

2. Dana Priest, "Private Guards Repel Attack on U.S. Headquarters," *Washington Post,* April 6, 2004.

Chapter 16

The (Iraq) War on Civil Liberties

Jules Lobel

War places enormous strains on our nation's civil liberties and legal system. Often repeated is the Roman maxim first coined by Cicero, "inter arma silent leges," usually interpreted as "The power of law is suspended during war." Late chief justice William H. Rehnquist reformulated Cicero's phrase, noting that the law is not quite silent during war—but speaks with "a somewhat different voice."[1] Or, as Franklin Delano Roosevelt's wartime attorney general starkly put it, "The Constitution has not greatly bothered any wartime President."[2]

The Iraq war has continued this tradition. But this war, perhaps more than any other in U.S. history, has been premised on an ideology that runs fundamentally contrary to the rule of law and civil liberties. As other chapters in this book have explored, it was a preventive war, launched not in self-defense against an attack or even imminent threat of attack from Iraq but to prevent a possible future attack. This preventive war in Iraq was connected to the Bush administration's adoption of a broader theory of prevention, claiming for the government the right to use highly coercive measures not only in response to some demonstrable wrongdoing by a foreign state or individual, but to prevent possible misconduct in the future. That approach is at the root of both the Iraq war and the administration's worst violations of civil liberties and human rights.

In the immediate aftermath of September 11, 2001, top White House lawyers determined "that [the administration] had to move from retribution and punishment to preemption and prevention."[3] Attorney General John Ashcroft characterized the Administration's new domestic law enforcement approach as a "new . . . paradigm of prevention,"[4] while the administration's new National Security Strategy announced what President Bush termed "a new doctrine called preemption."[5] The adoption of this new prevention paradigm was closely connected to the government's decision to initiate warfare in Afghanistan and Iraq, for as the White House lawyers meeting after September 11 agreed, "only a warfare model allows the approach."[6]

The Bush administration's turn to a new coercive preventive model led it to sacrifice human rights and civil liberties under cover of preventing future terrorist attacks. In the name of prevention, the administration locked up over 5,000 aliens in the aftermath of September 11 whom it suspected might be terrorists, many for weeks or months. The vast majority were never even charged with any terrorist crime, and none of those preventively detained stands today convicted of any terrorist crime. In the name of prevention, the government has pursued a policy of extraordinary rendition in which individuals the government suspects may be associated with terrorism are sent to countries known to torture detainees. The administration transformed the practice of extraordinary rendition from a method used to transfer accused criminals to another country for trial to a preventive technique in which suspects are sent to another country not for the purpose of bringing them to justice, but so that the other country may detain them and extract information deemed important to prevent future attacks. Innocent people like Maher Arar, a Canadian citizen sent to Syria, where he was detained for a year and tortured, or Khalid el-Masri, a German citizen sent to Afghanistan, have been ensnared in such "renditions."

In the name of prevention, the government has wiretapped thousands of American citizens without obtaining the warrants required by law. And in furtherance of the preventive paradigm, the government has employed a wide range of coercive interrogation tactics on prisoners in Iraq, Afghanistan, and Guantanamo, including sleep deprivation, stress positioning, extended exposure to extreme heat and cold, threatened attacks by dogs, and waterboarding, a process in which the suspect is tied to a bench, immersed in water, and made to feel that he or she is drowning. These inhumane, "alternative" interrogation techniques are defended on the grounds that they will obtain information necessary to prevent future terrorist attacks on American soldiers or civilians. In the name of prevention, the administration has preventively detained hundreds of suspected terrorists at Guantanamo Bay without providing them any semblance of due process of law. In the name of obtaining intelligence to prevent future attacks, the administration has also "disappeared" allegedly high-value al-Qaeda suspects into CIA "black sites"—prisons in undisclosed locations where the government's conduct is not subject to any outside scrutiny and the suspect is completely cut off from the outside world. None of these human rights abuses are isolated violations; rather they stem from the same "preventive" strategy that led the administration to assert the right to invade a country not to thwart an ongoing or imminent attack against us or our allies, but to prevent a possible future attack.

These methods are fundamentally at odds with the rule of law. Where the rule of law normally requires that the government only use coercive force on the basis of objective evidence of wrongdoing, the preventive paradigm relies on predictions and suspicions of future wrongdoing. Such predictions generally cannot be proved true or false. They frequently rest on questionable assumptions, stereotypes, and misconceptions, and are particularly vulnerable to pretextual manipulation. The administration's policies and actions have been guided by little more than "the principle of actionable suspicion," as one former intelligence chief called it. The "whole concept was that not having hard evidence shouldn't hold you back."[7]

Where the rule of law seeks clear rules evenhandedly applied, the preventive paradigm substitutes an ad hoc balancing test in which state coercive action is permitted when the magnitude of the potential harm is deemed great enough to justify it. Thus, the administration's 2002 National Security Strategy replaced the clear international law rules of self-defense with a vague balancing test in which the greater the threat, the less certainty is required about its probability. Where the rule of law requires checks on executive power, the preventive paradigm substitutes sweeping executive discretion. And where the rule of law requires fair and open procedures before coercive punitive measures can be imposed on an individual or another state, the preventive paradigm employs truncated, often secretive processes that deny individuals a meaningful opportunity to prove their innocence.

In sum, the coercive preventive model associated with both the Iraq war and human rights violations in the name of national security substitutes ad hoc balancing for clear rules, allows judgments based on suspicion rather than hard evidence, and discards legal checks on unilateral decision making. These elements sacrifice key components of what democratic nations have come to accept as the rule of law.

Just as the Iraq war was launched based on fears and suspicions rather than objective evidence, so too thousands of aliens have been preventively detained based on such easily manipulable suspicions. Just as U.S. officials inflated the evidence that Iraq had weapons of mass destruction, they inflated information they received from Canada in order to render Maher Arar to Syria, treating suspicion as if it were clear and unequivocal evidence. The United States bypassed the Security Council in its rush to initiate war against Iraq; so too the administration bypassed Congress in initiating warrantless surveillance of citizens.

The launching of the Iraq war represented an abuse of power by the Bush administration, ignoring world opinion strongly opposed to the war, disregarding the United Nations and the Security Council, and dismissing the work of the UN inspectors and of the International Atomic Energy Agency. The abuse of national power became the pretext for the administration's abuse of executive power at the expense of constitutional checks and balances. In reflecting on the Vietnam War, the prominent historian Henry Steele Commager noted that the "abuse of executive power cannot be separated from the abuse of national power. If we subvert world order and destroy world peace, we must inevitably subvert and destroy our own political institutions first."[8] What happened during the Vietnam War is recurring.

The Bush administration has claimed sweeping, inherent, and unchecked war powers that threaten to undermine our constitutional protections on individual liberty. It has argued that the president's inherent authority as commander in chief allows him to circumvent a congressional ban on torture or the cruel and inhumane treatment of detainees. The administration has also claimed that the president's inherent constitutional authority as commander in chief and the nation's sole organ of foreign affairs allows him to authorize warrantless wiretapping, irrespective of the Foreign Intelligence Surveillance Act (FISA). If FISA is read to prohibit the National Security Agency's warrantless wiretapping program (which it surely does), the administration argues that FISA, rather than the program, is unconstitutional. High-level administration advisors similarly claim that the president has the inherent authority to violate or suspend treaty provisions in wartime. The clearest and most sweeping statement of the president's authority came from the Department of Defense's Working Group Report on Detainee Interrogation in 2003, that "in wartime it is for the President alone to decide what methods to use to best prevail against the enemy."

These broad assertions of executive power bring to mind former president Richard Nixon's infamous remark "that when the President does it, that means that it is not illegal."[9]

Perhaps most dangerous is the administration's pursuit of a global war against terror that has no end. President Bush has not limited the war to defeating the insurgents in Iraq, the Taliban in Afghanistan, or even al-Qaeda. Rather he has claimed that the global war on terror will not "end until every terrorist group of global reach has been found, stopped and defeated."[10] Such an open-ended "war" against unnamed and future enemies threatens to undermine permanently our constitutional liberties, international human rights, and the checks and balances of a republic.

Notes

1. William H. Rehnquist, *All the Laws but One: Civil Liberties in Wartime* (New York: Random House, 1998), p. 225.

2. Ibid., p. 191.

3. Associate White House Counsel Bradford Berenson, quoted in Jane Mayer, "The Hidden Power," *New Yorker,* July 3, 2006.

4. John Ashcroft, Prepared Remarks Before the Council on Foreign Relations (February 10, 2003).

5. George W. Bush, Remarks at a Reception for Governor Tick Perry of Texas in Houston, PUB.990, 994 (June 14, 2002).

6. Mayer, "The Hidden Power."

7. Ron Suskind, *The One Percent Doctrine: Deep Inside America's Pursuit of Its Enemies Since 9/11* (New York: Simon and Schuster, 2006).

8. Henry Steele Commager, *The Defeat of America* (New York: Simon and Schuster, 1975).

9. *New York Times,* March 20, 1976, A16.

10. President George W. Bush, Transcript of President George W. Bush's Address to Congress, 9/20/2001.

Epilogue

War for Peace

C. K. Williams

Our violent men are more peaceful than your violent men.

Our violent men desire peace, only peace, they are passionately devoted to peace: your violent men desire only violence, which they pretend is a desire for peace.

Our violent men never lie, yours never speak truth. Therefore the pretended peace your violent men propose to attain through violence, unlike the peace our violent men propose, is not true peace at all but is merely an extension of their violence.[1]

Our violent men are compelled by spiritual considerations, while your violent men are devoted only to iniquity, and further violence; they are atheists or robotic fanatics. Our violent men partake of the holiness of our divinity, which consecrates their violence.

An essential element of the mission of our violent men is to make clear that only the divinity which defends us, and which they serve and defend, is worthy of being considered truly divine. Your divinity, because it is yours, is by definition less worthy than ours; therefore our violent men must honor our divinity and, in order to defend it from the ignoble divinity which deludes your violent men, must kill them.

However, our violent men have much less desire to kill than your violent men. Thus, when our violent men are compelled to slaughter other human beings, it is incidental to their real peaceful intentions.

Also, if some, or many, of those so slaughtered are not directly involved in the struggle against your violent men, that is to be considered an unfortunate necessity, and should not be particularly remarked. As a matter of fact, it would be gratuitous even to keep an accounting of these deaths.

In truth, our violent men believe that those who have had to die in our quest for our peaceful ends should consider themselves fortunate, should indeed be *grateful* for having been delivered from possible death by your violent men.

Our violent men are more powerful, more potent, than your violent men. They are exponentially more dedicated to our well-being than your violent men are to yours, and thus have need of greater resources than yours. It is therefore unreasonable to believe there should be a limit on the proportion of our resources relegated to the efficient functioning of our violent men. We cannot know precisely the resource-access of other violent men; hence, to continue adequately to defend ourselves against them, we must put at the disposition of our violent men any portion of our wealth and wherewithal they might deem they have need of, now or at any time in the future.

Our violent men are tirelessly vigilant, and demand of us a vigilance of our own. So sometimes our violent men will convey to us the necessity of initiating violence first, now, *now,* before other violent men, the stealthy, cowardly, deceitful, unscrupulous, treacherous other violent men are able to carry out their unthinkably nefarious plots against us. It is our absolute responsibility to support our violent men in this decision, as in any other decision at which they may arrive.

Some have found it strange that it is in the care of violent men that we have bestowed all but entirely our progress towards peace, that we have put in their care the very definition of peace, but this shouldn't be surprising; it has always been so. There have always been a sufficient number of us frightened by the mere possibility that alien violent men may usurp our own violent men's authority and bring down alien violence upon us, that they are eager to give over their sovereignty, their lives, the lives of their children, (especially their children), so as to not to suffer any longer from the possibility of such a dire eventuality.

Those who thus feel protected by our violent men understand that an enduring state of violence is preferable to sporadic outbreaks of peace, during which violence may be perpetrated on them without their having been prepared for it. If the state of violence in which we are allowed to participate means we will be subjected to an abiding anxiety and that sacrifices of other aspects of our existence will be demanded of us, it is to be considered a fair bargain.

It is self-evident then that in order to maintain this protection we must also put into the care of our violent men our system of laws. Because our violent men are so wholly dedicated to upholding our laws, the laws must be put at their service, otherwise a misinterpretation of the laws might impede the effort our violent men may have to make, or may already have made (it is not for us to know this) in their striving for peace.

In truth, we cannot be permitted to know, or know for certain, the degree of legality or lawlessness of the violence our violent men have implemented, nor which of the laws they have been forced to redefine in their striving towards peace.

This will ensure that our violent men will never have to admit having been *wrong*: they will never have to regret what might appear like failure, because this would surely be construed by other violent men as an admission of weakness, which will in fact *make us* weak, and thus bring the wrath of other violent men upon us.

There have been moments when *unviolent* men may seem to have usurped the prestige and authority of our violent men, but these have been the briefest aberrations. The world's violent men have always demonstrated that the state of unviolence thus postulated, precisely because it *is* unviolent, engenders danger and is to be mistrusted.

In a word, *security,* even a security which entails unflagging fear, is more to be wished for than any other condition of existence. This is why our violent men propose to us a state of insecurity which will never end, because of their benevolence towards and concern for us.

A benevolence and concern for which we must give thanks, unto death.

Note

1. Sometimes our violent men are of the female gender. This is of no moment; they are still violent men. Wombs and breasts are no impediment to the execution of violence, or its promulgation. Also, only a very few of our violent men participate in the actual enactment of violence. Most of our violent men

instead are *theoreticians* of violence, *conceivers* of violence, *planners* of violence, *propagandists* of violence, *executives* of violence, *producers of the means of* violence. All these violent men are more crucial to our peace than those who merely risk their lives to enact violence, and are accordingly more lavishly rewarded.

About the Contributors

Miriam Pemberton, Ph.D., is research fellow at the Institute for Policy Studies and Peace and Security editor of its Foreign Policy in Focus project. She leads the team that produces the annual "Unified Security Budget for the United States."

William D. Hartung is director of the Arms and Security Initiative at the New America Foundation. He is the author of *And Weapons for All* (HarperCollins, 1994) and *How Much Are You Making on the War, Daddy? A Quick and Dirty Guide to War Profiteering in the George W. Bush Administration* (Nation Books, 2005).

Fred Barbash is a lecturer at the Medill Washington Program at Northwestern University. He has served as national editor, London bureau chief, and Supreme Court correspondent at the *Washington Post*.

Phyllis Bennis is a fellow at the Institute for Policy Studies. She is the author, among other books, of *Before and After: U.S. Foreign Policy and the September 11th Crisis* (Interlink Press, 2002) and *Challenging Empire: How People, Governments, and the UN Defy U.S. Power* (Interlink Press, 2006).

Linda Bilmes teaches budgeting and public finance at the Kennedy School of Government at Harvard University. During the Clinton administration, she served as chief financial officer at the U.S. Department of Commerce. She is the author of "Soldiers Returning from Iraq and Afghanistan: The Long-Term Costs of Providing Veterans Medical Care and Disability Benefits" and, with Joseph E. Stiglitz, "The Economic Costs of the Iraq War: An Appraisal Three Years after the Beginning of the Conflict."

Hans Blix served from 1981 until 1997 as director general of the International Atomic Energy Agency and from January 2000 to June 2003 as the head of the United Nations Monitoring, Verification, and Inspection Commission. He has written several books on international and constitutional law.

Neta C. Crawford is professor of political science and African American studies at Boston University. She is the author of *Argument and Change in World Politics: Ethics, Decolonization, Humanitarian Intervention* (Cambridge University Press, 2002), which was a co-winner of the 2003 American Political Science Association Jervis and Schroeder Award for best book in international history and politics.

Ivan Eland is senior fellow at the Independent Institute, formerly director of defense policy studies at the Cato Institute, principal defense analyst at the Congressional Budget Office, evaluator-in-charge (national security and intelligence) for the U.S. General Accounting Office, and investigator for the House Foreign Affairs Committee. He is the author of *The Efficacy of Economic Sanctions as a Foreign Policy Tool* (1991).

Frances FitzGerald is a journalist and author, best known for her book, *Fire in the Lake: The Vietnamese and the Americans in Vietnam* (Little, Brown, 1972), which was awarded both a Pulitzer Prize and the National Book Award.

Aziz Huq is coauthor of *Unchecked and Unbalanced: Presidential Power in a Time of Terror* (New Press, 2007). He works at the Brennan Center for Justice at New York University School of Law and is a 2006 Carnegie Scholars Fellow.

Chalmers Johnson is professor emeritus at the University of California, San Diego. He has written numerous books, including, most recently, three examinations of the consequences of American Empire: *Blowback* (2000, Owl Books), *The Sorrows of Empire* (Metropolitan Books, 2004), and *Nemesis: The Last Days of the American Republic* (Metropolitan Books, 2007).

Michael Klare is a Five Colleges professor of peace and world security studies at Hampshire College and author of *Resource Wars* (Owl Books, 2002) and *Blood and Oil: The Dangers and Consequences of America's Growing Petroleum Dependency* (Metropolitan Books, 2005) and the forthcoming *Rising Powers, Shrinking Planet: The New Geopolitics of Energy* (Metropolitan Books, 2008).

Jeffrey Laurenti is a senior fellow and director of policy programs at the Century Foundation. He writes extensively on international security issues.

Jules Lobel teaches at the University of Pittsburgh Law School. He has conducted human rights investigations in Gaza and the West Bank in

Israel and testified before Congress. He is the author, with David Cole, of *Less Safe, Less Free: Why America Is Losing the War on Terror* (New Press, 2007).

John Prados is an analyst with the National Security Archive. He is the author of twelve books, including *Lost Crusader: The Secret Wars of CIA Director William Colby* (Oxford University Press, 2003) and *The White House Tapes* (New Press, 2003).

Anas Shallal is an Iraqi American restaurateur and artist and the founder of Iraqi Americans for Peaceful Alternatives.

Norman Solomon is the author of "MediaBeat," a column that critiques media coverage of foreign and domestic issues, and the author of *War Made Easy: How Presidents and Pundits Keep Spinning Us to Death* (John Wiley and Sons, 2005).

Joseph Stiglitz is an economist and professor at Columbia University. A former senior vice president and chief economist of the World Bank, he was the recipient of the 2001 Nobel Prize in Economics.

Janine Wedel is a professor of public policy at George Mason University. A four-time Fulbright fellow and recipient of awards from the National Science Foundation, the MacArthur Foundation, the Ford Foundation, the Woodrow Wilson International Center for Scholars, and the U.S. Institute of Peace, she is author of *Collision and Collusion: The Strange Case of Western Aid to Eastern Europe* (Macmillan, 2001).

C. K. Williams is the author of nine books of poetry, the most recent of which, *The Singing,* won the National Book Award for 2003. His previous book, *Repair,* was awarded the 2000 Pulitzer Prize, and his collection *Flesh and Blood* received the National Book Critics Circle Award. He teaches in the creative writing program at Princeton University.

Index